The Complete Healthy Cookbook for Beginners

1500 Days of Scrumptious and Heart-Friendly Recipes with a 28-Day Meal Plan to Nourish Your Body | Full Color Edition

Marlene E. Harris

Editor: AALIYAH LYONS

Interior Design: BROOKE WHITE

Cover Art: DANIELLE REES

Food stylist: Sienna Adams

Table Of Contents

Introduction

Diving into the vibrant tapestry of flavors and wellness, we proudly present this cookbook - a treasury of culinary delights thoughtfully assembled to nurture your heart and invigorate your taste buds. In a world where the path to health is paved with dietary choices, this cookbook emerges as a guiding compass, offering an array of recipes that are a testament to the inseparable connection between good food and cardiovascular vitality.

In the mosaic of modern nutrition, complexity often meets confusion, yet the power to forge a harmonious relationship with our bodies remains within our grasp. The recipes you'll uncover within these pages are more than a mere collection; they're a gateway to embracing heart-healthy living without compromising on the joy of eating.

This cookbook isn't just about food – it's a declaration of autonomy over our well-being, a proclamation that the journey to heart health can be a satisfying and delectable one. with each dish, we embark on a path that marries the thrill of culinary exploration with the wisdom of nurturing our hearts.

In a culinary world brimming with possibilities, the recipes in this collection underscore the art of crafting bold flavors from ingredients that love our hearts back. From salads that radiate with the hues of health, to entrées that unite taste and vitality, to desserts that redefine sweetness without sacrificing wellness – this compendium celebrates the spectrum of heart-conscious dining.

Inside these pages, you'll encounter recipes that spotlight lean proteins, whole grains, and a cornucopia of vegetables and fruits. You'll uncover the symphony of herbs and spices, not just as seasonings but as guardians of heart well-being. You'll witness how intelligent ingredient swaps and mindful cooking techniques can metamorphose dishes into heart-healthy indulgences, preserving the essence of gastronomic pleasure.

Behind every recipe lies a celebration of innovation. It's a tribute to the idea that nutritious dining isn't synonymous with deprivation; instead, it's an invitation to explore textures, flavors, and unions that excite the palate and rejuvenate the body. The Heart Healthy Cookbook unravels the myth that well-being requires sacrifice, highlighting the delightful harmony that transpires when nourishment and satisfaction entwine.

As you embark on this epicurean expedition, remember that the heart isn't just a biological entity; it symbolizes vibrancy, sentiment, and kinship. Sharing a meal with those you cherish magnifies the resonance of this cookbook's message. Let these recipes be a bridge that connects you with your own wellness and the wellness of those you hold dear.

Chapter 1

Healthy Eating, Healthy Heart

The Heart's Symbolism and Connection

Beyond its physical role as a vital organ, the heart has transcended its anatomical boundaries to become an enduring symbol of human emotion, connection, and life itself. From ancient civilizations to modern times, the heart has maintained its position as a universal emblem of love, compassion, and vulnerability. This symbolism extends further, intertwining with our culinary experiences, our shared meals, and our pursuit of heart-healthy living. The heart's profound resonance in these aspects of our lives is a testament to its enduring significance.

A SYMBOL OF EMOTION AND LOVE

The heart's connection to emotions traces back through history, spanning cultures and centuries. In ancient Egyptian beliefs, the heart was believed to be the center of human consciousness, housing both thoughts and feelings. Similarly, ancient Greek philosophers associated the heart with emotions and moral character. Over time, this metaphorical association between the heart and emotions gave rise to the notion of the heart as the locus of love. Today, we "wear our hearts on our sleeves," and an image of a heart is universally recognized as a symbol of affection, compassion, and profound emotion.

SHARED MEALS AND BONDING

Culinary traditions across cultures often revolve around the act of sharing meals, a ritual that transcends mere sustenance. This act, rooted in the heart of human interaction, holds the power to strengthen bonds, forge connections, and foster a sense of belonging. The dinner table becomes a sacred space where stories are shared, laughter resounds, and relationships are nourished alongside the food. The heart's symbolism extends to these moments, infusing them with a deeper significance.

Think about a family gathered around the table for a holiday feast, friends sharing stories over a cozy dinner, or a couple celebrating an anniversary at a romantic restaurant. In each of these scenarios, the heart's symbolic resonance adds an extra layer of meaning to the experience. The heart's beat becomes not just a physiological rhythm but also a metaphorical cadence of togetherness.

HEART-HEALTHY LIVING: NURTURING OURSELVES AND OTHERS

As we navigate the intricate realm of health and well-being, the heart's symbolism extends into the choices we make to care for our bodies and those of our loved ones. Heart-healthy living becomes a tribute to the heart's multi-faceted significance. Choosing nutritious foods, engaging in regular exercise, managing stress, and fostering emotional well-being all align with the heart's symbolism of love and care.

In the context of cooking and food choices, this symbolism takes on a unique flavor. Preparing meals that are not only delicious but also nourishing for the heart bridges the gap between literal and metaphorical resonance. Each thoughtfully chosen ingredient and each lovingly prepared dish become expressions of self-care and care for others.

WHERE SYMBOLISM MEETS REALITY

The heart's symbolism and connection are not mere abstractions; they are woven into the fabric of our lives, enriching our experiences and choices. It's in the heartbeats that quicken when we're excited, the warmth that spreads when we're content, and the vulnerability that arises when we connect with others. It's in the shared laughter around a table, the comfort of a home-cooked meal, and the commitment to nurturing our bodies.

In embracing heart-healthy living, we're not just tending to our physical well-being but also acknowledging the heart's deep significance in our existence. Whether we're cooking a nourishing meal, sharing it with loved ones, or making conscious choices for our health, we're participating in a narrative that spans generations and cultures—a narrative that celebrates the heart's enduring role as a symbol of connection, love, and life.

窗体顶端

What Is a Heart-Healthy Diet?

A heart-healthy diet is a nutritional approach that prioritizes foods and eating patterns known to support cardiovascular health. It's a way of eating that aims to reduce the risk of heart disease, stroke, and other related conditions by making conscious choices about what we consume. While individual dietary needs may vary, the core principles of a heart-healthy diet remain consistent, focusing on nutrient-rich foods that nourish the heart and the body.

EMPHASIS ON WHOLE, NUTRIENT-RICH FOODS

At the heart of a heart-healthy diet are whole, nutrient-dense foods. These include a variety of fruits and vegetables, whole grains, lean proteins, and healthy fats. Whole foods are rich in vitamins, minerals, fiber, and antioxidants that promote overall health while specifically supporting cardiovascular well-being. These foods provide sustained energy, regulate blood sugar levels, and contribute to maintaining healthy blood pressure.

BALANCING MACRONUTRIENTS

A balanced intake of macronutrients—carbohydrates, proteins, and fats—is crucial for heart health. Complex carbohydrates from whole grains, fruits, and vegetables provide steady energy and fiber that aids digestion and helps manage cholesterol levels. Lean proteins like fish, poultry, beans, and legumes offer essential amino acids without the excess saturated fat found in many animal products. Healthy fats, such as those from nuts, seeds, avocados, and olive oil, are a cornerstone of heart-healthy diets as they can help lower bad cholesterol levels and reduce inflammation.

Limiting Saturated and Trans Fats

A heart-healthy diet encourages the reduction of saturated and trans fats, which are known contributors to heart disease. Saturated fats are often found in red meat, full-fat dairy products, and certain tropical oils. Trans fats, often listed as partially hydrogenated oils on ingredient labels, are commonly found in processed and fried foods. Replacing these unhealthy fats with unsaturated fats from sources like nuts, seeds, and fatty fish can help improve cholesterol levels and protect heart health.

REDUCING SODIUM INTAKE

Excessive sodium intake is linked to high blood pressure, a major risk factor for heart disease. A heart-healthy diet prioritizes the consumption of whole, minimally processed foods and encourages the use of herbs, spices, and other flavor-enhancing ingredients in place of excessive salt. Reading labels and choosing lower-sodium options when available can further contribute to a heart-protective eating plan.

MODERATING ADDED SUGARS

High levels of added sugars in the diet are associated with obesity, type 2 diabetes, and heart disease. A heart-healthy diet aims to limit the consumption of sugary foods and beverages, instead favoring whole fruits for natural sweetness. This approach helps maintain stable blood sugar levels and reduces the risk of insulin resistance.

PROMOTING HYDRATION

Staying adequately hydrated is crucial for overall health and can have a positive impact on heart health. While water is the best choice for hydration, herbal teas and infused water with slices of fruits or herbs can be flavorful alternatives that don't contribute to added sugars or excessive calories.

The Importance of Heart-Healthy Eating

The heart, a tireless worker that beats approximately 100,000 times a day, serves as the engine that drives our entire body. Its ceaseless rhythm sustains life, making its health a paramount concern. The significance of heart-healthy eating extends far beyond the realm of maintaining a desirable weight or adhering to a passing dietary trend. It's a commitment to nurturing the very core of our existence, a conscious decision to honor the seat of our emotions and vitality with every bite we take. Understanding the importance of heart-healthy eating unveils a journey toward comprehensive well-being that encompasses both the physiological and emotional dimensions of our lives.

GUARDING AGAINST CARDIOVASCULAR DISEASES

Cardiovascular diseases, which include conditions like coronary artery disease, heart attacks, and strokes, remain leading causes of death worldwide. The foundation of heart-healthy eating lies in its power to reduce the risk factors associated with these ailments. A diet rich in whole grains, fruits, vegetables, lean proteins, and healthy fats helps maintain healthy blood pressure, cholesterol levels, and blood sugar. These factors play a pivotal role in shielding the heart from the damage that can lead to potentially life-threatening heart conditions.

PROMOTING OPTIMAL HEART FUNCTION

A heart-healthy diet supplies the essential nutrients required for optimal heart function. Nutrients such as omega-3 fatty acids, found in fatty fish like salmon, support heart health by reducing inflammation and improving blood vessel function. Antioxidants present in fruits and vegetables, such as vitamins C and E, help neutralize harmful free radicals that can damage cells and contribute to heart disease. Consuming a variety of nutrient-rich foods ensures that the heart receives the building blocks it needs to perform its vital role effectively.

MANAGING WEIGHT AND METABOLISM

Maintaining a healthy weight is integral to heart health, as excess weight places additional strain on the cardiovascular system. A heart-healthy diet not only provides essential nutrients but also encourages portion control and mindful eating. Whole foods, rich in fiber and water content, promote satiety, helping individuals manage their weight naturally. Furthermore, focusing on nutrient-dense options reduces the likelihood of overindulging in calorie-dense, processed foods that can contribute to weight gain and metabolic imbalances.

ELEVATING EMOTIONAL AND MENTAL WELL-BEING

The connection between the heart and emotions goes beyond metaphor. Science reveals that a diet rich in nutrients can positively influence mood and mental health. Omega-3 fatty acids, for instance, are not only beneficial for heart health but also for brain function and emotional well-being. Consuming nutrient-rich foods supports the production of neurotransmitters that regulate mood and stress responses, contributing to an overall sense of emotional equilibrium.

CULTIVATING HOLISTIC WELL-BEING

Heart-healthy eating transcends the boundaries of physical health, embracing a holistic approach to well-being. It recognizes the intricate interplay between the physical and emotional aspects of our lives. Eating with the heart's well-being in mind signifies an act of self-love, an acknowledgment of our responsibility to care for ourselves in the most comprehensive manner possible. It's an investment in long-term vitality and the ability to engage fully in life's experiences.

Tips for Eating Heart Healthy

In a world filled with tempting culinary indulgences, making heart-healthy choices might seem like a daunting task. However, prioritizing cardiovascular well-being doesn't have to be a sacrifice. with a bit of knowledge and thoughtful consideration, you can embark on a journey of heart-healthy eating that's both satisfying and sustainable. Here are some tips to guide you on this transformative path:

EMBRACE COLORFUL, PLANT-BASED FOODS

Fruits and vegetables are rich in vitamins, minerals, fiber, and antioxidants that nourish your heart and body. Aim to fill half your plate with a vibrant assortment of these plant-based foods. The array of colors represents a spectrum of nutrients that contribute to heart health.

OPT FOR WHOLE GRAINS

Replace refined grains with whole grains like brown rice, quinoa, whole wheat, and oats. Whole grains are high in fiber, which helps regulate blood sugar levels and reduce cholesterol. They provide sustained energy and a feeling of fullness, curbing unhealthy snacking.

PRIORITIZE LEAN PROTEINS

Choose lean protein sources such as poultry, fish, beans, lentils, and tofu. These options are lower in saturated fats than red meat, making them heart-friendlier choices. Fatty fish, like salmon and mackerel, also provide heart-protective omega-3 fatty acids.

BE MINDFUL OF FATS

Opt for healthy fats found in avocados, nuts, seeds, and olive oil. These fats support heart health by improving cholesterol levels and reducing inflammation. Limit saturated and trans fats found in fried foods, processed snacks, and fatty cuts of meat.

LIMIT SODIUM INTAKE

Excessive sodium consumption can contribute to high blood pressure, a major risk factor for heart disease. Be cautious with processed foods, canned soups, and restaurant meals, which often contain high levels of sodium. Choose herbs, spices, and other flavor enhancers to reduce the need for excessive salt.

CONTROL PORTION SIZES

Eating in moderation is key to preventing overconsumption of calories and maintaining a healthy weight. Be mindful of portion sizes, especially when dining out, as restaurants often serve larger portions than necessary.

PLAN BALANCED MEALS

Create balanced meals that include a variety of nutrients. Each meal should ideally consist of lean protein, whole grains, and an abundance of vegetables. This combination ensures you're getting a well-rounded dose of essential nutrients.

HYDRATE WISELY

Water is essential for overall health, including heart health. Opt for water, herbal teas, and infused water with slices of fruits and herbs to stay hydrated without unnecessary added sugars.

CHOOSE SNACKS WISELY

When snacking, reach for heart-healthy options like raw nuts, fresh fruits, and vegetables. These snacks provide fiber and nutrients to keep you satisfied between meals.

READ LABELS

Become a savvy label reader. Pay attention to nutrition labels, ingredient lists, and serving sizes. Look for foods low in saturated and trans fats, added sugars, and sodium.

COOK AT HOME

Cooking at home gives you control over ingredients and preparation methods. Experiment with heart-healthy recipes that incorporate fresh, whole foods.

PRACTICE MINDFUL EATING

Slow down and savor your meals. Pay attention to hunger and fullness cues, and avoid distractions while eating. Mindful eating promotes better digestion and prevents overeating.

ENJOY TREATS IN MODERATION

It's okay to indulge occasionally, but do so in moderation. If you're craving something sweet or indulgent, choose smaller portions or healthier alternatives.

STAY ACTIVE

Physical activity complements heart-healthy eating. Aim for regular exercise to strengthen your cardiovascular system and enhance overall well-being.

Chapter 2

Heart Health Made Easy

Kitchen Equipment Basics

Equipping your kitchen with the right tools is essential for efficient and enjoyable cooking experiences. Whether you're a novice or an experienced home cook, having the right kitchen equipment can make a significant difference in your culinary adventures. Here are some kitchen equipment basics that every well-stocked kitchen should have:

CHEF'S KNIFE

A sharp and versatile chef's knife is a kitchen essential for chopping, slicing, and dicing a variety of ingredients. Invest in a quality knife that feels comfortable in your hand.

CUTTING BOARD

A sturdy cutting board provides a safe and clean surface for food preparation. Opt for a board made of materials that are easy to clean and maintain.

MIXING BOWLS

Mixing bowls in various sizes are crucial for combining ingredients, tossing salads, and more. Stainless steel or glass bowls are durable options.

MEASURING TOOLS

Accurate measurements are essential for successful recipes. Have measuring cups and spoons on hand for both liquid and dry ingredients.

COOKWARE SET

A basic set of cookware, including pots and pans of various sizes, allows you to cook a wide range of dishes. Nonstick options are great for easy cleanup.

WOODEN SPOON AND SPATULA

These utensils are versatile for stirring, sautéing, and mixing without damaging your cookware's surface.

TONGS

Tongs are handy for flipping and turning items while cooking, especially on grills or stovetops.

BAKING SHEET AND PAN

Essential for roasting vegetables, baking cookies, and preparing sheet pan meals.

WHISK

Whisks are perfect for beating eggs, incorporating ingredients, and creating smooth sauces and batters.

COLANDER OR STRAINER

For draining pasta, rinsing produce, and separating liquids from solids.

CAN OPENER

A functional can opener is necessary for opening canned goods quickly and easily.

BLENDER OR FOOD PROCESSOR

These appliances are versatile for making smoothies, pureeing soups, and creating sauces.

TOASTER OR TOASTER OVEN

Ideal for quickly toasting bread, bagels, and reheating small meals.

PEELER

A vegetable peeler is essential for removing skin from fruits and vegetables.

GRATER

Graters are useful for shredding cheese, zesting citrus, and more.

OVEN MITTS

Protect your hands when handling hot pots, pans, and dishes from the oven.

KITCHEN TIMER

Keep track of cooking times accurately to prevent overcooking.

Heart-Healthy Foods to Enjoy

Prioritizing heart health doesn't mean sacrificing flavor or satisfaction. In fact, there's a plethora of delicious and nutrient-rich foods that can contribute to a thriving cardiovascular system. These heart-healthy foods are not only good for your body but also delightful for your taste buds. Incorporate these foods into your diet to nourish your heart while indulging in flavors you love:

BERRIES

Blueberries, strawberries, raspberries, and blackberries are packed with antioxidants, vitamins, and fiber. They can help lower blood pressure, improve blood vessel function, and reduce inflammation.

FATTY FISH

Salmon, mackerel, sardines, and trout are rich in omega-3 fatty acids. These fats have been shown to lower triglycerides, reduce the risk of arrhythmias, and decrease inflammation.

WHOLE GRAINS

Opt for whole grains like oats, quinoa, brown rice, and whole wheat. They're high in fiber, which helps lower cholesterol levels and stabilize blood sugar.

LEAFY GREENS

Spinach, kale, Swiss chard, and other leafy greens are abundant in vitamins, minerals, and antioxidants. They support heart health by reducing blood pressure and promoting overall cardiovascular function.

NUTS

Almonds, walnuts, pistachios, and other nuts provide healthy fats, fiber, and a range of beneficial nutrients. Enjoy them in moderation for heart-protective benefits.

LEGUMES

Beans, lentils, and chickpeas are excellent sources of plant-based protein and fiber. They help regulate blood sugar levels and reduce the risk of heart disease.

AVOCADO

This creamy fruit is a source of monounsaturated fats that can lower bad cholesterol levels. Avocados also contain potassium, which supports heart health by helping to regulate blood pressure.

DARK CHOCOLATE

In moderation, dark chocolate with a high cocoa content (70% or higher) contains antioxidants called flavonoids that can improve heart health by reducing blood pressure and improving blood flow.

OLIVE OIL

Rich in monounsaturated fats and antioxidants, extra virgin olive oil is a staple of Mediterranean diets and can help improve cholesterol levels and reduce inflammation.

GARLIC

Garlic contains compounds that have been linked to improved cardiovascular health. It may help lower blood pressure and reduce cholesterol levels.

FLAXSEEDS

These tiny seeds are a great source of omega-3 fatty acids, fiber, and lignans, which can help reduce blood pressure and inflammation.

OATS

Oats are rich in beta-glucans, a type of soluble fiber that can help lower cholesterol levels and improve heart health.

POMEGRANATE

Pomegranates are packed with antioxidants that have been shown to have anti-inflammatory effects and improve overall heart health.

GREEN TEA

Green tea is high in antioxidants called catechins, which have been associated with improved heart health and reduced risk of heart disease.

Foods to Be Wary of

As you embark on a journey to prioritize heart health, being mindful of your food choices is crucial. While there are many heart-healthy foods to embrace, there are also certain foods that can have a negative impact on your cardiovascular well-being. These are foods that are high in unhealthy fats, sodium, added sugars, and refined carbohydrates. By understanding which foods to be wary of, you can make informed choices that support your heart's vitality:

TRANS FATS

Trans fats are artificially created fats often found in processed and fried foods. They can raise bad cholesterol levels (LDL) and lower good cholesterol levels (HDL), increasing the risk of heart disease. Read ingredient labels and avoid products with "partially hydrogenated oils."

SUGARY SNACKS AND BEVERAGES

Foods and beverages high in added sugars, such as sugary cereals, candies, sugary drinks, and sweetened baked goods, contribute to weight gain and can increase the risk of heart disease and type 2 diabetes.

SATURATED FATS

Foods high in saturated fats, such as fatty cuts of meat, full-fat dairy products, and certain tropical oils like coconut oil, can raise LDL cholesterol levels. While some sources of saturated fats are okay in moderation, it's best to limit their consumption.

EXCESSIVE SODIUM

High sodium intake can contribute to high blood pressure, a risk factor for heart disease. Be cautious with salty snacks, canned soups, processed foods, and restaurant dishes, which often contain hidden sodium.

PROCESSED AND FAST FOODS

Processed foods are often high in unhealthy fats, added sugars, sodium, and artificial additives. Fast food, in particular, tends to be calorie-dense and nutrient-poor, contributing to weight gain and heart health concerns.

REFINED CARBOHYDRATES

Foods made with refined carbohydrates, such as white bread, white rice, and sugary cereals, can cause rapid spikes in blood sugar levels. Over time, this can lead to insulin resistance and an increased risk of heart disease.

HIGH-PROCESSED MEATS

Processed meats like bacon, sausages, hot dogs, and deli meats are high in sodium and unhealthy fats. They have been linked to an increased risk of heart disease, stroke, and certain types of cancer.

ARTIFICIAL TRANS FATS

Artificial trans fats are found in some commercially baked and fried foods. They not only raise bad cholesterol levels but also lower good cholesterol levels, making them doubly harmful to heart health.

HIGH-CALORIE, LOW-NUTRIENT FOODS

Foods that are high in calories but low in essential nutrients, such as many fast foods and sugary snacks, can contribute to weight gain and increase the risk of heart disease.

LARGE PORTIONS

Oversized portions can lead to overeating and weight gain, both of which are detrimental to heart health. Be mindful of portion sizes, especially when dining out.

SUGARY BREAKFAST CEREALS

Many breakfast cereals marketed to children are high in added sugars and lack the fiber and nutrients needed for a heart-healthy start to the day.

ALCOHOL IN EXCESS

While moderate alcohol consumption can have certain health benefits, excessive drinking can contribute to high blood pressure, heart disease, and other health issues.

Popular Heart-Healthy Eating Patterns

When it comes to promoting heart health, dietary choices play a pivotal role. Several well-researched eating patterns have emerged as effective ways to support cardiovascular well-being. These patterns not only emphasize wholesome foods but also encourage mindful eating habits. Among the most popular and widely studied are the Mediterranean diet, the DASH (Dietary Approaches to Stop Hypertension) diet, and vegetarian/vegan diets. Let's explore each of these heart-healthy eating patterns in detail.

• Mediterranean Diet

The Mediterranean diet is inspired by the traditional dietary patterns of countries bordering the Mediterranean Sea. It's characterized by an abundance of whole, minimally processed foods, with an emphasis on plant-based ingredients, healthy fats, and moderate consumption of lean protein sources.

KEY COMPONENTS:

- Fruits and Vegetables: A variety of colorful fruits and vegetables provide essential vitamins, minerals, and antioxidants.
- Whole Grains: Whole grains like whole wheat, quinoa, and brown rice offer fiber and sustained energy.
- Healthy Fats: Olive oil is a primary source of healthy monounsaturated fats, while nuts, seeds, and fatty fish provide omega-3 fatty acids.
- Lean Proteins: Poultry, fish, and legumes are favored over red meat, promoting heart health.
- Moderate Wine Consumption: Red wine, in moderation, is often enjoyed with meals for its potential heart-protective properties.
- Herbs and Spices: Flavorful herbs and spices are used in place of excess salt for seasoning.
- Limited Processed Foods: Processed foods, sugary treats, and sugary beverages are minimized.

The Mediterranean diet's emphasis on whole foods, healthy fats, and plant-based ingredients contributes to its reputation as a heart-healthy eating pattern. Research suggests that it can help reduce the risk of heart disease, lower cholesterol levels, and improve overall cardiovascular well-being.

• DASH Diet

The DASH diet was developed as a dietary approach to manage hypertension (high blood pressure). It focuses on reducing sodium intake while promoting a well-balanced intake of essential nutrients.

KEY COMPONENTS:

• Fruits and Vegetables: High intake of fruits and vegetables provides potassium, magnesium, and fiber.
• Whole Grains: Whole grains offer essential nutrients and fiber for heart health.
• Lean Proteins: Lean meats, poultry, fish, and plant-based protein sources like beans and nuts are recommended.
• Dairy: Low-fat or fat-free dairy products provide calcium and other nutrients.
• Nuts and Seeds: Nuts, seeds, and legumes contribute healthy fats and protein.
• Limited Sodium: The DASH diet encourages reducing sodium intake to manage blood pressure.
• Moderate Sweets: Limited consumption of sweets and added sugars is advised.

The DASH diet's focus on nutrient-rich foods, potassium, and reduced sodium intake makes it effective in managing blood pressure and reducing the risk of heart disease. It also promotes overall balanced nutrition, which supports cardiovascular health.

• Vegetarian/Vegan Diets

Vegetarian and vegan diets are centered around plant-based foods and exclude or significantly limit animal products. These diets can promote heart health by emphasizing nutrient-dense, fiber-rich foods.

KEY COMPONENTS:

• Plant-Based Foods: Fruits, vegetables, whole grains, legumes, nuts, and seeds are the foundation of these diets.
• Lean Proteins: Plant-based protein sources such as beans, lentils, tofu, and tempeh are emphasized.
• Healthy Fats: Nuts, seeds, avocados, and olive oil provide healthy fats.
• Limited Animal Products: Vegetarians may include some dairy and/or eggs, while vegans exclude all animal products.
• Supplements: Vegans often require supplementation of vitamin B12 and possibly other nutrients.

Vegetarian and vegan diets are associated with reduced risk factors for heart disease, including lower cholesterol levels and blood pressure. Their focus on plant-based foods and the exclusion of saturated fats found in some animal products contribute to their heart-healthy reputation.

A HEARTFELT APPROACH TO HEALTH

These heart-healthy eating patterns are more than just diets; they represent comprehensive approaches to nourishing your body and supporting your cardiovascular well-being. Each pattern encourages a shift toward whole, nutrient-dense foods while minimizing processed and unhealthy options. Ultimately, the key to success lies in finding an eating pattern that aligns with your preferences, lifestyle, and health goals. By embracing one of these heart-healthy eating patterns, you can embark on a journey of proactive heart care that brings not only physical benefits but also a sense of fulfillment and well-being.

Chapter 3

28-Day Meal Plan

Week 1

Welcome to the first week of your transformative heart-healthy diet plan. As you embark on this journey, remember that every step you take is a significant stride toward a healthier, more vibrant you. Week 1 is about embracing the new flavors and ingredients that will nourish your heart and invigorate your well-being. Begin by exploring the vibrant world of fruits and vegetables, savoring the array of colors and tastes that nature offers. Let this week be a gentle introduction to the path you're embarking upon—a path that promises better health and a renewed sense of vitality.

Meal Plan	Breakfast	Snack	Lunch	Dinner	Snack
Day-1	Baked Pear Pancake	Cherry Chocolate Cake	Salsa Verde Chicken	Pork Roulades	Cherry Chocolate Cake
	Calories: 129 | Total Fat: 2.0 g | Carbohydrates: 24 g| Fiber: 2 g |Protein: 5 g	Calories: 173 | Total Fat: 4g| Carbohydrates: 31g | Fiber: 5g | Protein: 6g	Calories: 257 | Total Fat: 5g | Carbohydrates: 14g | Fiber: 4g | Protein: 34g	Calories: 298 | Total Fat: 14.0 g |Carbohydrates: 10 g| Fiber: 2 g | Protein: 33 g	Calories: 173 | Total Fat: 4g| Carbohydrates: 31g | Fiber: 5g | Protein: 6g
Day-2	Baked Pear Pancake	Cherry Chocolate Cake	Salsa Verde Chicken	Pork Roulades	Cherry Chocolate Cake
	Calories: 129 | Total Fat: 2.0 g | Carbohydrates: 24 g| Fiber: 2 g |Protein: 5 g	Calories: 173 | Total Fat: 4g| Carbohydrates: 31g | Fiber: 5g | Protein: 6g	Calories: 257 | Total Fat: 5g | Carbohydrates: 14g | Fiber: 4g | Protein: 34g	Calories: 298 | Total Fat: 14.0 g |Carbohydrates: 10 g| Fiber: 2 g | Protein: 33 g	Calories: 173 | Total Fat: 4g| Carbohydrates: 31g | Fiber: 5g | Protein: 6g
Day-3	Baked Pear Pancake	Cherry Chocolate Cake	Salsa Verde Chicken	Pork Roulades	Cherry Chocolate Cake
	Calories: 129 | Total Fat: 2.0 g | Carbohydrates: 24 g| Fiber: 2 g |Protein: 5 g	Calories: 173 | Total Fat: 4g| Carbohydrates: 31g | Fiber: 5g | Protein: 6g	Calories: 257 | Total Fat: 5g | Carbohydrates: 14g | Fiber: 4g | Protein: 34g	Calories: 298 | Total Fat: 14.0 g |Carbohydrates: 10 g| Fiber: 2 g | Protein: 33 g	Calories: 173 | Total Fat: 4g| Carbohydrates: 31g | Fiber: 5g | Protein: 6g

Day-4	Baked Pear Pancake	Cherry Chocolate Cake	Salsa Verde Chicken	Pork Roulades	Cherry Chocolate Cake
	Calories: 129 | Total Fat: 2.0 g | Carbohydrates: 24 g| Fiber: 2 g |Protein: 5 g	Calories: 173 | Total Fat: 4g| Carbohydrates: 31g | Fiber: 5g | Protein: 6g	Calories: 257 | Total Fat: 5g | Carbohydrates: 14g | Fiber: 4g | Protein: 34g	Calories: 298 | Total Fat: 14.0 g |Carbohydrates: 10 g| Fiber: 2 g | Protein: 33 g	Calories: 173 | Total Fat: 4g| Carbohydrates: 31g | Fiber: 5g | Protein: 6g
Day-5	Baked Pear Pancake	Cherry Chocolate Cake	Salsa Verde Chicken	Pork Roulades	Cherry Chocolate Cake
	Calories: 129 | Total Fat: 2.0 g | Carbohydrates: 24 g| Fiber: 2 g |Protein: 5 g	Calories: 173 | Total Fat: 4g| Carbohydrates: 31g | Fiber: 5g | Protein: 6g	Calories: 257 | Total Fat: 5g | Carbohydrates: 14g | Fiber: 4g | Protein: 34g	Calories: 298 | Total Fat: 14.0 g |Carbohydrates: 10 g| Fiber: 2 g | Protein: 33 g	Calories: 173 | Total Fat: 4g| Carbohydrates: 31g | Fiber: 5g | Protein: 6g

Shopping List for Week 1

PROTEINS:

- 2 pounds boneless, skinless chicken breasts
- 2 1-pound pork tenderloins, all visible fat discarded, cut into 6 3 × 4-inch rectangles, then flattened to ¼-inch thickness
- 2 large egg whites
- 1 large egg

VEGETABLES:

- 1 bell pepper (any color), chopped
- 8 ounces button mushrooms
- 1 tablespoon chopped onion

FRUITS:

- 1 large ripe but firm pear, peeled and thinly sliced
- 2 cups salsa verde
- 1 (14.5-ounce) can no-salt-added fire-roasted tomatoes
- 1 (4-ounce) can green chiles
- 1 cup unsweetened dried cherries

NUTS:

- ¼ cup chopped walnuts

MISCELLANEOUS:

- 1 tablespoon sugar and 2 tablespoons plus 1 teaspoon sugar, divided use
- ¼ teaspoon ground cinnamon
- ⅛ teaspoon ground cloves
- 2 teaspoons canola or corn oil
- ¾ cup fat-free milk
- ½ cup all-purpose flour
- ¼ cup ground flaxseed
- 2 teaspoons baking powder
- ¼ teaspoon salt
- 2 tablespoons extra-virgin olive oil
- 1 tablespoon vanilla extract
- ½ cup granulated sugar
- ½ cup nonfat vanilla Greek yogurt
- ¾ cup low-fat or fat-free milk, or plant-based milk, divided
- 2 tablespoons all-purpose flour
- ½ cup fat-free, low-sodium beef broth
- 1 tablespoon canola or corn oil

Week 2

As you enter Week 2, you're already on your way to a heart-healthy lifestyle. This week, focus on nourishing your body from within. Experiment with heart-loving fats found in nuts, seeds, and avocados. Allow the omega-3-rich grace of fatty fish to grace your plate. You'll find that these ingredients not only satisfy your taste buds but also nurture your cardiovascular system. Your dedication to this journey is inspiring; remember that every choice you make aligns with your goal of supporting your heart's vitality.

Meal Plan	Breakfast	Snack	Lunch	Dinner	Snack
Day-1	Breakfast Meat Patties	Frosted Cake	Sesame-Orange Salmon	Philadelphia-Style Cheese Steak Wrap	Frosted Cake
	Calories: 100 | Total Fat: 4.0 g | Carbohydrates: 3 g| Fiber: 0 g | Protein: 13 g	Calories: 241| Total Fat: 5g| Protein: 4g| Carbohydrates: 45g	Calories: 235 | Total Fat: 10.5 g | Carbohydrates: 5 g| Fiber: 1 g | Protein: 29 g	Calories: 173 | Total Fat: 2.5 g | Carbohydrates: 18 g| Fiber: 3 g | Protein: 19 g	Calories: 241| Total Fat: 5g| Protein: 4g| Carbohydrates: 45g
Day-2	Breakfast Meat Patties	Frosted Cake	Sesame-Orange Salmon	Philadelphia-Style Cheese Steak Wrap	Frosted Cake
	Calories: 100 | Total Fat: 4.0 g | Carbohydrates: 3 g| Fiber: 0 g | Protein: 13 g	Calories: 241| Total Fat: 5g| Protein: 4g| Carbohydrates: 45g	Calories: 235 | Total Fat: 10.5 g | Carbohydrates: 5 g| Fiber: 1 g | Protein: 29 g	Calories: 173 | Total Fat: 2.5 g | Carbohydrates: 18 g| Fiber: 3 g | Protein: 19 g	Calories: 241| Total Fat: 5g| Protein: 4g| Carbohydrates: 45g
Day-3	Breakfast Meat Patties	Frosted Cake	Sesame-Orange Salmon	Philadelphia-Style Cheese Steak Wrap	Frosted Cake
	Calories: 100 | Total Fat: 4.0 g | Carbohydrates: 3 g| Fiber: 0 g | Protein: 13 g	Calories: 241| Total Fat: 5g| Protein: 4g| Carbohydrates: 45g	Calories: 235 | Total Fat: 10.5 g | Carbohydrates: 5 g| Fiber: 1 g | Protein: 29 g	Calories: 173 | Total Fat: 2.5 g | Carbohydrates: 18 g| Fiber: 3 g | Protein: 19 g	Calories: 241| Total Fat: 5g| Protein: 4g| Carbohydrates: 45g

Day-4	Breakfast Meat Patties	Frosted Cake	Sesame-Orange Salmon	Philadelphia-Style Cheese Steak Wrap	Frosted Cake
	Calories: 100 | Total Fat: 4.0 g | Carbohydrates: 3 g| Fiber: 0 g | Protein: 13 g	Calories: 241| Total Fat: 5g| Protein: 4g| Carbohydrates: 45g	Calories: 235 | Total Fat: 10.5 g | Carbohydrates: 5 g| Fiber: 1 g | Protein: 29 g	Calories: 173 | Total Fat: 2.5 g | Carbohydrates: 18 g| Fiber: 3 g | Protein: 19 g	Calories: 241| Total Fat: 5g| Protein: 4g| Carbohydrates: 45g
Day-5	Breakfast Meat Patties	Frosted Cake	Philadelphia-Style Cheese Steak Wrap	Philadelphia-Style Cheese Steak Wrap	Frosted Cake
	Calories: 100 | Total Fat: 4.0 g | Carbohydrates: 3 g| Fiber: 0 g | Protein: 13 g	Calories: 241| Total Fat: 5g| Protein: 4g| Carbohydrates: 45g	Calories: 173 | Total Fat: 2.5 g | Carbohydrates: 18 g| Fiber: 3 g | Protein: 19 g	Calories: 173 | Total Fat: 2.5 g | Carbohydrates: 18 g| Fiber: 3 g | Protein: 19 g	Calories: 241| Total Fat: 5g| Protein: 4g| Carbohydrates: 45g

Shopping List for Week 2

PROTEINS:

- 1 pound extra-lean ground beef
- 4 salmon fillets with skin (about 5 ounces each) or 4 skinless salmon fillets (about 4 ounces each), rinsed and patted dry
- 12 ounces eye-of-round roast, all visible fat discarded, cut diagonally across the grain into ⅛-inch slices
- 4 eggs

VEGETABLES:

- 1 small onion, thinly sliced

- 1 medium green bell pepper, thinly sliced
- 2 medium garlic cloves, minced

FRUITS:

- 2 tablespoons fresh orange juice and ½ cup fresh orange juice, divided use

NUTS:

- 3 tablespoons sesame seeds

MISCELLANEOUS:

- ½ cup fat-free, low-sodium beef broth
- ¼ cup fine dry bread crumbs (lowest sodium available)
- 2 teaspoons grated lemon zest
- 1 tablespoon fresh lemon juice
- ¼ teaspoon dried sage
- ¼ teaspoon ground ginger
- 2 teaspoons canola or corn oil
- Cooking spray
- 1 teaspoon soy sauce (lowest sodium available)
- ½ teaspoon toasted sesame oil
- 1 tablespoon balsamic vinegar or red wine vinegar
- 2 teaspoons Worcestershire sauce (lowest sodium available)
- 1 teaspoon sugar
- 1 teaspoon dried oregano, crumbled
- 1 teaspoon olive oil
- 2¼ cups cake flour
- 2¼ tsp baking powder
- 1¼ cups sugar
- 4 tbsp margarine
- 1 tbsp orange peel
- 1 tsp vanilla
- ¾ cup skim milk
- 3 oz low-fat cream cheese
- 2 tbsp skim milk
- 6 tbsp cocoa
- 2 cups confectioners' sugar, sifted

Week 3

Week 3 invites you to savor every bite and fully embrace the art of mindful eating. As you explore new recipes and cooking techniques, take a moment to appreciate the nourishment you're providing for your body. Listen to your body's cues and eat with intention, relishing each mouthful. This week is about more than just food—it's about cultivating a positive relationship with what you consume. Your commitment to mindful eating is commendable, and the benefits you'll reap extend far beyond your plate.

Meal Plan	Breakfast	Snack	Lunch	Dinner	Snack
Day-1	Strawberry Yogurt Tarts	Crunchy Pumpkin Pie	Greek Fish Fillets	Mexican Fried Rice	Crunchy Pumpkin Pie
	Calories: 141kcal| Fat: 5g| Carbs: 20g| Protein: 5g	Calories: 169| Total Fat: 7g| Fiber: 3g| Protein: 5g| Carbohydrates: 22g	Calories: 153 | Total Fat: 6.5 g |Carbohydrates: 1 g| Fiber: 0 g | Protein: 23 g	Calories: 149 | Total Fat: 1.0 g | Carbohydrates: 30 g| Fiber: 2 g | Protein: 3 g	Calories: 169| Total Fat: 7g| Fiber: 3g| Protein: 5g| Carbohydrates: 22g

Day-2	Strawberry Yogurt Tarts	Crunchy Pumpkin Pie	Greek Fish Fillets	Mexican Fried Rice	Crunchy Pumpkin Pie
	Calories: 141kcal| Fat: 5g| Carbs: 20g| Protein: 5g	Calories: 169| Total Fat: 7g| Fiber: 3g| Protein: 5g| Carbohydrates: 22g	Calories: 153 | Total Fat: 6.5 g |Carbohydrates: 1 g| Fiber: 0 g | Protein: 23 g	Calories: 149 | Total Fat: 1.0 g | Carbohydrates: 30 g| Fiber: 2 g | Protein: 3 g	Calories: 169| Total Fat: 7g| Fiber: 3g| Protein: 5g| Carbohydrates: 22g
Day-3	Strawberry Yogurt Tarts	Crunchy Pumpkin Pie	Greek Fish Fillets	Mexican Fried Rice	Crunchy Pumpkin Pie
	Calories: 141kcal| Fat: 5g| Carbs: 20g| Protein: 5g	Calories: 169| Total Fat: 7g| Fiber: 3g| Protein: 5g| Carbohydrates: 22g	Calories: 153 | Total Fat: 6.5 g |Carbohydrates: 1 g| Fiber: 0 g | Protein: 23 g	Calories: 149 | Total Fat: 1.0 g | Carbohydrates: 30 g| Fiber: 2 g | Protein: 3 g	Calories: 169| Total Fat: 7g| Fiber: 3g| Protein: 5g| Carbohydrates: 22g
Day-4	Strawberry Yogurt Tarts	Crunchy Pumpkin Pie	Greek Fish Fillets	Mexican Fried Rice	Crunchy Pumpkin Pie
	Calories: 141kcal| Fat: 5g| Carbs: 20g| Protein: 5g	Calories: 169| Total Fat: 7g| Fiber: 3g| Protein: 5g| Carbohydrates: 22g	Calories: 153 | Total Fat: 6.5 g |Carbohydrates: 1 g| Fiber: 0 g | Protein: 23 g	Calories: 149 | Total Fat: 1.0 g | Carbohydrates: 30 g| Fiber: 2 g | Protein: 3 g	Calories: 169| Total Fat: 7g| Fiber: 3g| Protein: 5g| Carbohydrates: 22g
Day-5	Strawberry Yogurt Tarts	Berry Banana Smoothie	Mexican Fried Rice	Mexican Fried Rice	Berry Banana Smoothie
	Calories: 141kcal| Fat: 5g| Carbs: 20g| Protein: 5g	Calories: 133 | Total Fat: 0.5 g |Sodium: 3 mg | Carbohydrates: 32 g| Fiber: 3 g | Protein: 2 g	Calories: 149 | Total Fat: 1.0 g | Carbohydrates: 30 g| Fiber: 2 g | Protein: 3 g	Calories: 149 | Total Fat: 1.0 g | Carbohydrates: 30 g| Fiber: 2 g | Protein: 3 g	Calories: 133 | Total Fat: 0.5 g |Sodium: 3 mg | Carbohydrates: 32 g| Fiber: 3 g | Protein: 2 g

Shopping List for Week 3

PROTEINS:
- 4 thin fish fillets, such as tilapia, (about 4 ounces each), rinsed and patted dry
- 1 egg, beaten

VEGETABLES:
- 1 medium lemon, cut into 4 wedges
- 1 medium garlic clove, minced
- ⅔ cup canned chopped green chiles, drained
- 4 to 5 medium green onions, thinly sliced

FRUITS:
- ½ cup strawberries
- 1 cup strawberries, hulled and halved, or raspberries
- 1 medium banana, cut into large pieces
- 1 teaspoon canola or corn oil
- 2 tablespoons water

NUTS:
- ½ cup crushed almonds
- ¼ cup ground almonds

MISCELLANEOUS:
- ½ cup pitted Medjool dates
- 1 tablespoon maple syrup
- 1 teaspoon dried oregano, crumbled
- 1 teaspoon salt-free lemon pepper
- ¼ teaspoon paprika
- ¼ teaspoon salt
- Cooking spray
- 1 tablespoon plus 1 teaspoon olive oil (extra-virgin preferred)
- 1 cup uncooked long-grain rice
- 2 cups fat-free, low-sodium chicken broth
- 1 cup quick cooking oats
- ¼ cup whole wheat flour
- 2 tbsp brown sugar
- ¼ tsp salt
- 3 tbsp vegetable oil
- 1 tbsp water
- ¼ cup brown sugar, packed
- ½ tsp ground cinnamon
- ¼ tsp ground nutmeg
- 4 tsp vanilla
- 1 cup canned pumpkin
- 2/3 cup evaporated skim milk
- 1 cup 100% orange juice

Week 4

Congratulations on reaching Week 4 of your heart-healthy diet plan! You've embarked on a transformative journey, and now is the time to celebrate your progress. This week, reflect on how far you've come and embrace the positive changes you've incorporated into your life. Continue to enjoy the nourishing recipes and heart-healthy ingredients that have become a part of your routine. As you complete this month-long plan, remember that this isn't just a temporary endeavor—it's a foundation for lasting well-being. Your persistence, dedication, and newfound knowledge empower you to continue making heart-conscious choices long into the future. The journey you've embarked upon is one of self-care, self-discovery, and a deep commitment to your heart's health. You've proven that you have the strength to prioritize your well-being, and your heart will thank you for it every day.

Meal Plan	Breakfast	Snack	Lunch	Dinner	Snack
Day-1	Cinnamon-Nutmeg Bread	Dark Chocolate Walnut Cookies	Mini Crab Casseroles	Kung Pao Chicken	Spiced Baked Apples
	Calories: 106 | Total Fat: 2.0 g | Carbohydrates: 19 g| Fiber: 2 g | Protein: 3 g	Calories: 83 | Total Fat: 4.0 g | Carbohydrates: 11 g| Fiber: 1 g | Protein: 2 g	Calories: 118 | Total Fat: 1.0 g | Carbohydrates: 10 g| Fiber: 1 g | Protein: 16 g	Calories: 312 | Total Fat: 8g | Carbohydrates: 24g | Fiber: 4g | Protein: 36g	Calories: 240 | Total Fat: 8g | Carbohydrates: 42g | Fiber: 7g | Protein: 3g
Day-2	Cinnamon-Nutmeg Bread	Dark Chocolate Walnut Cookies	Mini Crab Casseroles	Kung Pao Chicken	Spiced Baked Apples
	Calories: 106 | Total Fat: 2.0 g | Carbohydrates: 19 g| Fiber: 2 g | Protein: 3 g	Calories: 83 | Total Fat: 4.0 g | Carbohydrates: 11 g| Fiber: 1 g | Protein: 2 g	Calories: 118 | Total Fat: 1.0 g | Carbohydrates: 10 g| Fiber: 1 g | Protein: 16 g	Calories: 312 | Total Fat: 8g | Carbohydrates: 24g | Fiber: 4g | Protein: 36g	Calories: 240 | Total Fat: 8g | Carbohydrates: 42g | Fiber: 7g | Protein: 3g
Day-3	Cinnamon-Nutmeg Bread	Dark Chocolate Walnut Cookies	Mini Crab Casseroles	Kung Pao Chicken	Spiced Baked Apples
	Calories: 106 | Total Fat: 2.0 g | Carbohydrates: 19 g| Fiber: 2 g | Protein: 3 g	Calories: 83 | Total Fat: 4.0 g | Carbohydrates: 11 g| Fiber: 1 g | Protein: 2 g	Calories: 118 | Total Fat: 1.0 g | Carbohydrates: 10 g| Fiber: 1 g | Protein: 16 g	Calories: 312 | Total Fat: 8g | Carbohydrates: 24g | Fiber: 4g | Protein: 36g	Calories: 240 | Total Fat: 8g | Carbohydrates: 42g | Fiber: 7g | Protein: 3g
Day-4	Cinnamon-Nutmeg Bread	Dark Chocolate Walnut Cookies	Mini Crab Casseroles	Kung Pao Chicken	Spiced Baked Apples
	Calories: 106 | Total Fat: 2.0 g | Carbohydrates: 19 g| Fiber: 2 g | Protein: 3 g	Calories: 83 | Total Fat: 4.0 g | Carbohydrates: 11 g| Fiber: 1 g | Protein: 2 g	Calories: 118 | Total Fat: 1.0 g | Carbohydrates: 10 g| Fiber: 1 g | Protein: 16 g	Calories: 312 | Total Fat: 8g | Carbohydrates: 24g | Fiber: 4g | Protein: 36g	Calories: 240 | Total Fat: 8g | Carbohydrates: 42g | Fiber: 7g | Protein: 3g

Day-5	Cinna-mon-Nut-meg Bread	Spiced Baked Apples	Mini Crab Casseroles	Kung Pao Chicken	Spiced Baked Apples
	Calories: 106 | Total Fat: 2.0 g | Carbohydrates: 19 g| Fiber: 2 g | Protein: 3 g	Calories: 240 | Total Fat: 8g | Carbohydrates: 42g | Fiber: 7g | Protein: 3g	Calories: 118 | Total Fat: 1.0 g | Carbohydrates: 10 g| Fiber: 1 g | Protein: 16 g	Calories: 312 | Total Fat: 8g | Carbohydrates: 24g | Fiber: 4g | Protein: 36g	Calories: 240 | Total Fat: 8g | Carbohydrates: 42g | Fiber: 7g | Protein: 3g

Shopping List for Week 4

PROTEINS:

- 3 cups flaked crabmeat, thawed if frozen or rinsed and drained if canned, bits of shell and cartilage discarded
- 2 pounds boneless, skinless chicken breast, cut into 1-inch pieces
- 1 large egg
- 1 large egg, well beaten

VEGETABLES:

- 2 tablespoons minced onion
- 1 medium rib of celery, finely chopped, or ¼ teaspoon celery seeds
- 2 celery stalks, chopped
- 1 red bell pepper, chopped
- 1 green bell pepper, chopped
- 4 medium carrots, sliced
- 2 cups snow peas

FRUITS:

- 6 apples

NUTS:

- ⅓ cup chopped almonds
- 1 cup chopped walnuts, dry-roasted

MISCELLANEOUS:

- Cooking spray
- ⅔ cup sugar
- ¼ cup light tub margarine

- ¼ cup unsweetened applesauce
- 2 cups sifted white whole-wheat flour
- 1 teaspoon ground cinnamon
- 1 teaspoon ground nutmeg
- ½ teaspoon baking powder
- ½ teaspoon baking soda
- 1 cup low-fat buttermilk
- ½ teaspoon canola or corn oil
- 1 2-ounce jar diced pimientos, drained
- 2 tablespoons minced green bell pepper
- 1 tablespoon chopped fresh parsley
- Dash of red hot-pepper sauce
- 2 tablespoons dry sherry
- ¼ cup egg substitute
- 2 slices whole-grain bread (lowest sodium available), lightly toasted and crumbled
- ¼ cup low-sodium soy sauce
- ¼ cup balsamic vinegar
- 4 tablespoons sriracha sauce (or to taste)
- 4 garlic cloves, minced
- 2 tablespoons honey (or to taste)
- 1 tablespoon freshly grated ginger
- 1 tablespoon sesame oil
- 2 tablespoons cornstarch
- ½ cup light brown sugar
- 3 tablespoons light tub margarine, softened
- 1 teaspoon vanilla, butter, and nut flavoring or vanilla extract
- ¾ cup self-rising flour
- ⅓ cup unsweetened cocoa powder
- ½ cup apple juice
- 2 tablespoons extra-virgin olive oil

Chapter 4

Breakfast

Cinnamon-Nutmeg Bread

Prep time: 10 minutes | Cook time: 58 minutes | Serves 16

- Cooking spray
- ⅔ cup sugar
- ¼ cup light tub margarine
- 1 large egg, well beaten
- ¼ cup unsweetened applesauce
- 2 cups sifted white whole-wheat flour
- 1 teaspoon ground cinnamon
- 1 teaspoon ground nutmeg
- ½ teaspoon baking powder
- ½ teaspoon baking soda
- 1 cup low-fat buttermilk

1. Preheat the oven to 350°F. Lightly spray a 9 × 5 × 3-inch loaf pan with cooking spray.
2. In a large mixing bowl, using an electric mixer on medium speed, beat the sugar and margarine for 2 to 3 minutes, or until creamed. Add the egg and applesauce. Beat until the mixture is well blended.
3. Put the remaining ingredients except the buttermilk in a medium bowl. Sift together twice.
4. Alternately add the flour mixture and buttermilk to the sugar mixture, beginning and ending with the flour and stirring after each addition until the mixture is moistened, but no flour is visible. Pour the batter into the loaf pan, gently smoothing the top.
5. Bake for 45 minutes to 1 hour, or until a wooden toothpick inserted in the center comes out clean. Let cool in the pan for 10 minutes. Using a metal spatula, loosen the bread from the sides of the pan. Turn out onto a cooling rack. Let cool completely.

PER SERVING

Calories: 106 | Total Fat: 2.0 g | Saturated Fat: 0.0 g | Trans Fat: 0.0 g | Polyunsaturated Fat: 0.5 g | Monounsaturated Fat: 1.0 g | Cholesterol: 12 mg | Sodium: 95 mg | Carbohydrates: 19 g| Fiber: 2 g | Sugars: 10 g | Protein: 3 g

Strawberry Yogurt Tarts

Prep time: 15 minutes |Cook time: 0 minute |Serves 5

½ cup pitted medjool dates
½ cup crushed almonds
1 tablespoon maple syrup
1 cup low-fat plain greek yogurt
½ cup strawberries
2 tablespoons water

1. Line 5 cups of a muffin tin with paper liners and set aside.
2. In a food processor or blender, place the dates and pulse for 10 to 20 seconds until they become a paste.
3. Add the crushed almonds and maple syrup to the blender and pulse to mix.
4. Evenly divide the date mixture into the lined cups and press it firmly; it should fill about one-third of the cup.
5. Blend the yogurt, strawberries, and water in a clean blender until smooth.
6. Pour the fruit and yogurt mixture into the cups until each one is full.
7. Bring the cups to the freezer for 2 hours to set and serve.

PER SERVING:

Calories: 141kcal| Fat: 5g| Carbs: 20g| Protein: 5g

Apricot-Orange Bread

Prep time: 8 minutes | Cook time: 65 minutes | Serves 2

- 1 package (6 oz) dried apricots, cut into small pieces
- 1 cup sugar
- 2 tbsp margarine
- 1 egg, slightly beaten
- 1 tbsp orange peel, freshly grated
- 3½ cups all-purpose flour, sifted
- ½ cup fat-free dry milk powder
- 2 tsp baking powder
- 1 tsp baking soda
- 1 tsp salt
- ½ cup orange juice
- ½ cup pecans, chopped

1. Preheat oven to 350°F. Lightly oil two, 9-by 5-inch loaf pans.
2. Cook apricots in 2 cups of water in covered medium-size saucepan for 10 to 15 minutes or until tender but not mushy. Drain and reserve ¾ cup liquid. Set apricots aside to cool.
3. Cream together sugar and margarine. By hand, beat in egg and orange peel.
4. Sift together flour, dry milk, baking powder, baking soda, and salt. Add to creamed mixture alternately with reserved apricot liquid and the orange juice.
5. Stir apricot pieces and pecans into batter.
6. Turn batter into prepared pans.
7. Bake for 40 to 45 minutes or until bread springs back when lightly touched in center.
8. Cool for 5 minutes in pans. Remove from pans and completely cool on wire rack before slicing.

PER SERVING:

Calories: 97| Total Fat: 2g| Saturated Fat: less than 1g| Cholesterol: 6mg| Sodium: 113mg| Total Fiber: 1g| Protein: 2g| Carbohydrates: 18g| Potassium: 110mg

Breakfast Meat Patties

Prep time: 10 minutes | Cook time: 23 minutes | Serves 8

- 1 pound extra-lean ground beef
- ½ cup fat-free, low-sodium beef broth
- ¼ cup fine dry bread crumbs (lowest sodium available)
- 2 teaspoons grated lemon zest
- 1 tablespoon fresh lemon juice
- ¼ teaspoon dried sage
- ¼ teaspoon ground ginger
- 2 teaspoons canola or corn oil

1. In a large bowl, using your hands or a spoon, combine all the ingredients except the oil. Let stand for 15 minutes so the flavors blend.
2. Form into 8 patties about ¼ inch thick. Transfer the patties to a large plate.
3. In a large, heavy skillet, heat the oil over medium heat, swirling to coat the bottom. Cook the patties for 7 or 8 minutes on each side, or until browned on the outside and no longer pink in the center.

PER SERVING

Calories: 100 | Total Fat: 4.0 g | Saturated Fat: 1.5 g | Trans Fat: 0.0 g | Polyunsaturated Fat: 0.5 g | Monounsaturated Fat: 2.0 g | Cholesterol: 31 mg | Sodium: 70 mg | Carbohydrates: 3 g| Fiber: 0 g | Sugars: 0 g | Protein: 13 g

Cranberry Bread

Prep time: 10 minutes | Cook time: 50 minutes | Serves 16

- Cooking spray
- 2 cups white whole-wheat flour
- ⅔ cup firmly packed light brown sugar
- 2 teaspoons baking powder
- ½ teaspoon baking soda
- ¼ teaspoon ground allspice or ground nutmeg
- ⅛ teaspoon salt
- 1 cup fresh or frozen cranberries, chopped (don't thaw if frozen)
- 2 teaspoons grated orange zest
- ¾ cup fresh orange juice
- ¼ cup egg substitute
- 1 tablespoon canola or corn oil
- 2 teaspoons vanilla extract

1. Preheat the oven to 350°F. Lightly spray an 8 ½ × 4 ½ × 2 ½-inch loaf pan with cooking spray.
2. In a large bowl, sift together the flour, brown sugar, baking powder, baking soda, allspice, and salt. Make a well in the center.
3. In a medium bowl, stir together the remaining ingredients. Pour into the well. Stir just until the dry ingredients are moistened but no flour is visible. Don't overmix; the batter should be slightly lumpy. Pour into the loaf pan, gently smoothing the top.
4. Bake for 50 minutes to 1 hour, or until a wooden toothpick inserted in the center comes out clean. Using a metal spatula, loosen the bread from the sides of the pan. Turn out onto a cooling rack. Let cool before slicing.

PER SERVING

Calories: 105 | Total Fat: 1.0 g | Saturated Fat: 0.0 g | Trans Fat: 0.0 g | Polyunsaturated Fat: 0.5 g | Monounsaturated Fat: 0.5 g | Cholesterol: 0 mg | Sodium: 118 mg | Carbohydrates: 20 g| Fiber: 2 g | Sugars: 11 g | Protein: 3 g

Baked Pear Pancake

Prep time: 10 minutes | Cook time: 23 minutes | Serves 6

- 1 large ripe but firm pear, peeled and thinly sliced
- 1 tablespoon sugar and 2 tablespoons plus 1 teaspoon sugar, divided use
- ¼ teaspoon ground cinnamon
- ⅛ teaspoon ground cloves
- 2 teaspoons canola or corn oil
- ¾ cup fat-free milk
- ½ cup all-purpose flour
- 3 large egg whites
- ¼ cup egg substitute
- ½ teaspoon vanilla extract
- ⅛ teaspoon salt
- 2 teaspoons confectioners' sugar

1. Preheat the oven to 425°F.
2. Put the pear slices, 1 tablespoon sugar, the cinnamon, and cloves in a medium bowl. Gently stir together to coat.
3. In a 10-inch ovenproof nonstick or cast iron skillet, heat the oil over medium-high heat, swirling to coat the bottom. Arrange the pear slices in a single layer in the skillet. Cook for 5 minutes, or until beginning to soften (don't stir).

PER SERVING

Calories: 129 | Total Fat: 2.0 g | Saturated Fat: 0.0 g | Trans Fat: 0.0 g | Polyunsaturated Fat: 0.5 g | Monounsaturated Fat: 1.0 g | Cholesterol: 1 mg | Sodium: 110 mg | Carbohydrates: 24 g| Fiber: 2 g | Sugars: 13 g | Protein: 5 g

Chapter 5

Appetizers, Snacks, and Beverages

Luscious Berry Dip

Prep time: 10 minutes | Cook time: none | Serves 8

- 1 cup fat-free ricotta cheese
- ¾ cup halved fresh strawberries, hulled, or ¾ cup frozen strawberries, thawed
- ½ cup fresh raspberries, or ¾ cup frozen unsweetened raspberries, thawed, undrained
- ¼ cup fat-free vanilla yogurt
- 1 tablespoon light brown sugar
- ½ teaspoon ground cinnamon

1. In a food processor or blender, process all the ingredients until smooth. \
2. Transfer to a small serving bowl. Cover and refrigerate until ready to serve.

PER SERVING

Calories: 45 | Total Fat: 0.0 g | Saturated Fat: 0.0 g | Trans Fat: 0.0 g | Polyunsaturated Fat: 0.0 g | Monounsaturated Fat: 0.0 g | Cholesterol: 3 mg | Sodium: 66 mg | Carbohydrates: 6 g| Fiber: 1 g | Sugars: 5 g | Protein: 5 g

Cardamom Apple Almond Crisp

Prep time: 10 minutes | Cook time: 25 minutes | Serves 4

Olive oil nonstick cooking spray

For The Fruit
- 2 cups chopped unpeeled apples
- ½ tablespoon brown sugar
- 1 teaspoon cornstarch
- ¼ teaspoon ground cardamom
- ½ teaspoon vanilla extract

For The Topping
- 4 tablespoons almonds
- 3 tablespoons gluten-free rolled oats
- 1 teaspoon olive oil
- 1 tablespoon brown sugar
- 1 teaspoon honey
- Pinch salt
- Preheat the oven to 400°F and grease two 8-ounce ramekins with cooking spray.

To Prepare The Fruit
1. In a medium bowl, stir together the apples, brown sugar, cornstarch, cardamom, and vanilla.

To Make The Topping
1. In a food processor, process the almonds until finely chopped. Add the oats and pulse until just chopped.
2. In a small bowl, add the olive oil, brown sugar, honey, and a pinch of salt.

To Prepare The Crisp
1. Add 2 tablespoons of the topping mixture into the fruit mixture and stir to combine.
2. Divide the fruit mixture between the prepared ramekins. Sprinkle the rest of the topping over the fruit mixture.
3. Cover the ramekins with their lids or loosely cover with aluminum foil (the tops will burn if left uncovered).
4. Bake for 22 to 25 minutes and cool slightly, uncovered, before serving.

PER SERVING

Calories: 279 | Fats: 9g | Protein: 4g | Cholesterol: 0mg | Carbohydrates: 50g | Fiber: 8g | Sodium: 82mg

Frosted Cake

Prep time: 10 minutes | Cook time: 55 minutes | Serves 16

- 2¼ cups cake flour
- 2¼ tsp baking powder
- 1¼ cups sugar
- 4 tbsp margarine
- 4 eggs
- 1 tbsp orange peel
- 1 tsp vanilla
- ¾ cup skim milk
- 3 oz low-fat cream cheese
- 2 tbsp skim milk
- 6 tbsp cocoa
- 2 cups confectioners' sugar, sifted
- ½ tsp vanilla extract

1. Preheat oven to 325°F
2. Grease 10-inch round pan (at least 2½ inches high) with small amount of cooking oil or use nonstick cooking oil spray. Powder pan with flour. Tap out excess flour.
3. Sift together flour and baking powder.
4. In separate bowl, beat together sugar and margarine until soft and creamy.
5. Beat in eggs, orange peel, and vanilla.
6. Gradually add flour mixture, alternating with milk, beginning and ending with flour.
7. Pour mixture into pan. Bake for 40 to 45 minutes or until done. Let cake cool for 5 to 10 minutes before removing from pan. Let cool completely before icing.
8. Cream together cream cheese and milk until smooth. Add cocoa. Blend well.
9. Slowly add sugar until icing is smooth. Mix in vanilla.
10. Smooth icing over top and sides of cooled cake.

PER SERVING:

Calories: 241| Total Fat: 5g| Saturated Fat: 2g| Cholesterol: 57mg| Sodium: 273mg| Total Fiber: 1g| Protein: 4g| Carbohydrates: 45g| Potassium: 95mg

Berry Banana Smoothie

Prep time: 10 minutes | Cook time: none | Serves 2

- 1 cup strawberries, hulled and halved, or raspberries
- 1 medium banana, cut into large pieces
- 1 cup 100% orange juice

1. In a food processor or blender, process all the ingredients until smooth.

PER SERVING

Calories: 133 | Total Fat: 0.5 g | Saturated Fat: 0.0 g | Trans Fat: 0.0 g | Polyunsaturated Fat: 0.0 g | Monounsaturated Fat: 0.0 g | Cholesterol: 0 mg | Sodium: 3 mg | Carbohydrates: 32 g| Fiber: 3 g | Sugars: 21 g | Protein: 2 g

Mango Shake

Prep time: 5 minutes | Cook time: 7 minutes | Serves 4

- 2 cups low-fat milk
- 4 tbsp frozen mango juice (or 1 fresh mango, pitted)
- 1 small banana
- 2 ice cubes

1. Put all ingredients into blender. Blend until foamy. Serve immediately.
2. Instead of mango juice, try orange, papaya, or strawberry juice.

PER SERVING:

Calories: 106| Total Fat: 2g| Saturated Fat: 1g| Cholesterol: 5mg| Sodium: 63mg| Total Fiber: 2g| Protein: 5g| Carbohydrates: 20g| Potassium: 361mg

Crunchy Pumpkin Pie

Prep time: 15 minutes | Cook time: 55 minutes | Serves 9

- 1 cup quick cooking oats
- ¼ cup whole wheat flour
- ¼ cup ground almonds
- 2 tbsp brown sugar
- ¼ tsp salt
- 3 tbsp vegetable oil
- 1 tbsp water
- ¼ cup brown sugar, packed
- ½ tsp ground cinnamon
- ¼ tsp ground nutmeg
- ¼ tsp salt
- 1 egg, beaten
- 4 tsp vanilla
- 1 cup canned pumpkin
- 2/3 cup evaporated skim milk

1. Preheat oven to 425°F
2. Mix oats, flour, almonds, sugar, and salt in small mixing bowl.
3. Blend oil and water in measuring cup with fork or small wire whisk until blended.
4. Add oil mixture to dry ingredients and mix well. If needed, add small amount of water to hold mixture together.
5. Press into 9-inch pie pan, and bake for 8 to 10 minutes, or until light brown.
6. Turn down oven to 350°F
7. Mix sugar, cinnamon, nutmeg, and salt in bowl.
8. Add egg and vanilla, and mix to blend ingredients.
9. Add pumpkin and milk, and stir to combine.
10. Pour filling into prepared pie shell.
11. Bake for 45 minutes at 350°F or until knife inserted near center comes out clean.

PER SERVING:

Calories: 169| Total Fat: 7g| Saturated Fat: 1g| Cholesterol: 24mg| Sodium: 207mg| Total Fiber: 3g| Protein: 5g| Carbohydrates: 22g| Potassium: 223mg

Mexican Potato Skins

Prep time: 10 minutes | Cook time: 1 hour 25 minutes | Serves 4

- 8 potato-skin quarters from Baked Potato Soup, or 2 8-ounce baked potato skins
- 2 tablespoons plus 2 teaspoons fat-free sour cream
- 8 fresh cilantro leaves, finely chopped
- ¼ cup salsa (lowest sodium available), such as Salsa Cruda
- 1 small fresh jalapeño, seeds and ribs discarded, thinly sliced

1. Preheat the oven to 400°F.
2. Place the potato skins on a baking sheet.
3. Bake for 8 to 10 minutes, or until hot and crisp. For extra-crisp skins, use a toaster oven (the time is the same as for the oven). Transfer to a plate.
4. Meanwhile, in a small bowl, stir together the sour cream and cilantro.
5. Spoon the salsa onto each potato skin. Top with a dollop of the sour cream mixture and the jalapeño slices.

PER SERVING

Calories: 38 | Total Fat: 0.0 g | Saturated Fat: 0.0 g | Trans Fat: 0.0 g | Polyunsaturated Fat: 0.0 g | Monounsaturated Fat: 0.0 g | Cholesterol: 2 mg | Sodium: 68 mg | Carbohydrates: 8 g| Fiber: 0 g | Sugars: 1 g | Protein: 1 g

Go Fish Snack Mix

Prep time: 10 minutes | Cook time: 1 minutes | Serves 16

- 2 ¼ cups baked whole-grain fish-shaped snack crackers
- ⅔ cup walnut halves, dry-roasted
- Cooking spray
- ¾ teaspoon apple pie spice
- 12 ounces dried mixed fruit (any combination)

1. In a large nonstick saucepan or skillet, stir together the fish crackers and walnuts. Lightly spray with cooking spray. Sprinkle with the apple pie spice. Cook over medium heat for 1 minute, or until the fish crackers are slightly warmed, stirring constantly.
2. Stir in the dried fruit. Remove from the heat. Spread the mixture on a baking sheet or large platter to cool. Serve immediately or refrigerate in an airtight container for up to five days.

PER SERVING

Calories: 114 | Total Fat: 4.0 g | Saturated Fat: 0.5 g | Trans Fat: 0.0 g | Polyunsaturated Fat: 2.5 g | Monounsaturated Fat: 1.0 g | Cholesterol: 0 mg | Sodium: 86 mg | Carbohydrates: 18 g| Fiber: 2 g | Sugars: 8 g | Protein: 2 g

Coconut Halibut Bites

Prep time: 10 minutes | Cook time: 8 minutes | Serves 12

Cooking spray
- ¼ cup egg substitute
- ½ teaspoon dried dillweed, crumbled
- ⅛ teaspoon pepper
- ¼ cup all-purpose flour
- ¼ cup sweetened shredded coconut
- 1 pound halibut fillets, rinsed and patted dry, cut into 24 1-inch cubes

Sauce
- ½ cup sweet orange marmalade
- 1 teaspoon grated lime zest
- 1 tablespoon fresh lime juice
- 1 tablespoon fresh lemon juice

1. Preheat the oven to 400°F. Lightly spray a baking sheet with cooking spray.
2. In a small shallow dish, whisk together the egg substitute, dillweed, and pepper. In a separate small shallow dish, stir together the flour and coconut. Set the dishes and baking sheet in a row, assembly-line fashion. Working in batches, put the fish in the egg substitute mixture, turning to coat. Using a slotted spoon, transfer the fish to the flour mixture, turning to coat and gently shaking off any excess. Place the fish on the baking sheet, spacing the cubes slightly apart so they brown evenly.
3. Bake for 7 to 8 minutes, or until the fish flakes easily when tested with a fork.
4. Meanwhile, in a small serving bowl, whisk together the sauce ingredients. Serve with the fish.

PER SERVING

Calories: 87 | Total Fat: 1.0 g | Saturated Fat: 0.5 g | Trans Fat: 0.0 g | Polyunsaturated Fat: 0.0 g | Monounsaturated Fat: 0.0 g | Cholesterol: 19 mg | Sodium: 44 mg | Carbohydrates: 12 g| Fiber: 0 g | Sugars: 8 g | Protein: 8 g

Chapter 6

Soups and Salads

Roasted Corn Soup

Prep time: 10 minutes | Cook time: 30 minutes | Serves 4

- Cooking spray
- 1 cup frozen whole-kernel corn, partially thawed
- 1 cup fat-free, low-sodium beef broth
- 1 cup chopped onion
- 1 medium garlic clove, minced
- 1¾ cups water
- 1 cup low-sodium mixed-vegetable juice
- 2 medium carrots, chopped
- ¼ large red bell pepper, chopped
- ¼ small green bell pepper, chopped
- 1 teaspoon chili powder
- ½ teaspoon ground cumin
- 2 tablespoons chopped fresh cilantro

1. Preheat the oven to 425°F.
2. Lightly spray a baking sheet with cooking spray. Spread the corn in a single layer on the baking sheet. Lightly spray the corn with cooking spray.
3. Roast for 12 to 14 minutes, or until lightly browned, stirring once halfway through. Remove from the oven.
4. About the time you stir the corn, stir together the broth, onion, and garlic in a medium saucepan. Cook over medium-high heat for 4 minutes.
5. Stir in the corn and the remaining ingredients except the cilantro. Reduce the heat to medium and cook for 15 minutes, stirring occasionally. Just before serving, stir in the cilantro.

PER SERVING

Calories: 95 | Total Fat: 0.5 g | Saturated Fat: 0.0 g | Trans Fat: 0.0 g | Polyunsaturated Fat: 0.5 g | Monounsaturated Fat: 0.0 g | Cholesterol: 0 mg | Sodium: 87 mg | Carbohydrates: 21 g| Fiber: 4 g | Sugars: 8 g | Protein: 4 g

Three-Bean Salad

Prep time: 10 minutes | Cook time: 8 minutes | Serves 14

- 10 ounces frozen or 1 pound fresh green beans, trimmed and halved
- 10 ounces frozen or 1 pound fresh yellow beans, trimmed and halved
- ½ cup cider vinegar
- ½ cup sugar
- ⅓ cup canola or corn oil
- ½ teaspoon pepper (freshly ground preferred)
- 1 medium garlic glove, minced
- 1 15.5-ounce can no-salt-added kidney beans, rinsed and drained
- 1 medium red onion, thinly sliced
- ½ medium bell pepper, any color, chopped

1. In a large saucepan, steam the green and yellow beans for 6 to 8 minutes, or just until tender-crisp. Transfer to a colander. Rinse with cold water to stop the cooking process. Let cool to room temperature. Drain well. Dry on paper towels.
2. Meanwhile, in a small saucepan, heat the vinegar and sugar over medium heat, stirring until the sugar is dissolved. Stir in the oil, pepper, and garlic.
3. In a large bowl, add the green and yellow beans, kidney beans, onion, bell pepper, vinegar, and dressing, tossing to combine.
4. Cover and chill for 6 hours or overnight so the flavors blend.

PER SERVING

Calories: 122 | Total Fat: 5.5 g | Saturated Fat: 0.5 g | Trans Fat: 0.0 g | Polyunsaturated Fat: 1.5 g | Monounsaturated Fat: 3.5 g | Cholesterol: 0 mg | Sodium: 26 mg | Carbohydrates: 16 g| Fiber: 3 g | Sugars: 9 g | Protein: 3 g

Minestrone Soup

Prep time: 15 minutes | Cook time: 7 to 8 hours on low | Serves 6 to 8

- 6 cups savory vegetable broth or low-sodium vegetable broth
- 1 (28-ounce) can no-salt-added diced tomatoes
- 1 (14.5-ounce) can white kidney beans, drained and rinsed
- 1 (14.5-ounce) can red kidney beans, drained and rinsed
- 2 large onions, chopped
- 3 celery stalks, chopped
- 2 carrots, chopped
- 1 medium zucchini, diced
- 1½ cups fresh green beans, trimmed and cut into ½-inch pieces
- 1 cup chopped fresh spinach
- ½ cup hulled barley
- 4 garlic cloves, minced
- 1 tablespoon chopped fresh parsley
- freshly ground black pepper

1. Combine all the ingredients in a 6-quart slow cooker. Cover and cook on low for 7 to 8 hours.
2. Serve warm.

PER SERVING

Calories: 254 | Total Fat: 0g | Saturated Fat: 0g | Trans Fat: 0g | Polyunsaturated Fat: 0g | Monounsaturated Fat: 0g | Cholesterol: 0mg | Sodium: 188mg | Carbohydrates: 52g | Fiber: 13g | Sugars: 11g | Protein: 12g

Farmers' Market Vegetable Soup

Prep time: 15 minutes | Cook time: 7 to 8 hours on low | Serves 6 to 8

- 4 medium potatoes such as yukon gold, cut into 1-inch cubes
- 2 cups peeled and cubed butternut squash (about 1½ pounds)
- 2 small yellow squash or zucchini, sliced
- 4 celery stalks, chopped
- 3 large carrots, chopped
- 1 medium onion, chopped
- 4 garlic cloves, peeled
- ¼ cup packed fresh cilantro
- ¼ cup packed fresh basil leaves
- 2 tablespoons extra-virgin olive oil
- 6 cups savory vegetable broth or low-sodium vegetable broth
- ⅛ teaspoon salt
- freshly ground black pepper
- 4 cups baby spinach
- juice of ½ lemon

1. Put the potatoes, butternut squash, yellow squash, celery, and carrots in a 6-quart slow cooker.
2. Place the onion, garlic, cilantro, basil, and olive oil into a food processor. Blend until it achieves a coarse and chunky consistency. Pour this into the slow cooker.
3. Next add the broth, salt, and pepper and stir to combine. Cover and cook on low for 7 to 8 hours.
4. Stir in the spinach and lemon juice about 30 minutes before serving.
5. Serve warm.

PER SERVING

Calories: 200 | Total Fat: 5g | Saturated Fat: 1g | Trans Fat: 0g | Polyunsaturated Fat: 1g | Monounsaturated Fat: 3g | Cholesterol: 0mg | Sodium: 256mg | Carbohydrates: 37g | Fiber: 8g | Sugars: 8g | Protein: 5g

Marinated Tomato Salad

Prep time: 10 minutes | Cook time: 20 minutes | Serves 6

- ¼ cup olive oil (extra-virgin preferred)
- 2 tablespoons balsamic vinegar or red wine vinegar
- 12 medium grape tomatoes (yellow preferred), halved
- ¼ cup thinly sliced red onion
- 6 kalamata olives, chopped
- 4 medium beefsteak tomatoes, thickly sliced
- ¼ cup chopped fresh mint
- ¼ teaspoon pepper, or to taste (freshly ground preferred)
- ⅛ teaspoon salt

1. In a medium bowl, whisk together the oil and vinegar. Stir in the grape tomatoes, onion, and olives. Let stand, covered, for about 20 minutes, stirring occasionally.
2. Arrange the sliced tomatoes on a serving platter. Spoon the grape tomato mixture over the sliced tomatoes. Sprinkle with the mint, pepper, and salt.

PER SERVING

Calories: 119 | Total Fat: 10.5 g | Saturated Fat: 1.5 g | Trans Fat: 0.0 g | Polyunsaturated Fat: 1.0 g | Monounsaturated Fat: 7.5 g | Cholesterol: 0 mg | Sodium: 125 mg | Carbohydrates: 6 g| Fiber: 2 g | Sugars: 4 g | Protein: 1 g

Roasted German Potato Salad

Prep time: 10 minutes | Cook time: 35 minutes | Serves 4

- Cooking spray
- 12 ounces baby red potatoes (about 5), cut into eighths (about 1-inch pieces)
- ½ teaspoon olive oil and ½ teaspoon olive oil, divided use
- 2 slices turkey bacon, chopped
- ¾ cup chopped onion
- 1 cup loosely packed spinach, stems discarded

- ¼ teaspoon caraway seeds

Dressing

- 1 tablespoon chopped fresh chives
- 2 teaspoons olive oil (extra-virgin preferred)
- 1 teaspoon cider vinegar
- ½ teaspoon spicy brown mustard
- ¼ teaspoon pepper

1. Preheat the oven to 425°F. Lightly spray a small rimmed baking sheet with cooking spray.
2. Put the potatoes in a medium bowl. Lightly spray the potatoes with cooking spray. Stir to coat. Arrange in a single layer on the baking sheet.
3. Roast for 25 minutes, or until the potatoes are golden brown and tender when pierced with the tip of a sharp knife.
4. Meanwhile, in a medium nonstick skillet, heat ½ teaspoon oil over medium heat, swirling to coat the bottom. Cook the bacon for 2 minutes, stirring occasionally.
5. Stir in the onion and the remaining ½ teaspoon oil. Cook for 3 to 4 minutes, or until the bacon is lightly browned and the onion is soft, stirring frequently.
6. Add the spinach. Cook for 2 to 3 minutes, or until the spinach is wilted. Remove from the heat.

PER SERVING

Calories: 126 | Total Fat: 5.0 g | Saturated Fat: 1.0 g | Trans Fat: 0.0 g | Polyunsaturated Fat: 1.0 g | Monounsaturated Fat: 3.0 g | Cholesterol: 5 mg | Sodium: 155 mg | Carbohydrates: 17 g| Fiber: 2 g | Sugars: 2 g | Protein: 4 g

Chapter 7

Seafood

Ginger-Soy Fillets

Prep time: 10 minutes | Cook time: 13 minutes | Serves 4

- 2 tablespoons all-purpose flour
- 4 firm white fish fillets (about 4 ounces each), rinsed and patted dry
- 1 tablespoon canola or corn oil
- 2 tablespoons sherry or fresh orange juice
- 1 teaspoon ground ginger
- 1 teaspoon soy sauce (lowest sodium available)
- ½ teaspoon sugar
- 1 medium garlic clove, minced
- 2 medium tomatoes, chopped
- 1 tablespoon chopped fresh parsley
- 2 teaspoons chopped chives or green onions (green part only)
- Pepper to taste (freshly ground preferred)

1. Put the flour in a shallow dish. Dip the fish in the flour, turning to coat and gently shaking off any excess. Transfer to a plate.
2. In a large, heavy skillet, heat the oil over medium-high heat, swirling to coat the bottom. Cook the fish for 4 minutes, or until slightly browned, turning once halfway through.
3. In a 1-cup measuring cup, whisk together the sherry, ginger, soy sauce, sugar, and garlic with enough water to make 1 cup. Pour over the fish. Cook, covered, for 6 minutes.
4. Sprinkle the remaining ingredients over the fish. Cook, uncovered, for 3 minutes, or until the fish flakes easily when tested with a fork.

PER SERVING

Calories: 161 | Total Fat: 4.5 g | Saturated Fat: 0.5 g | Trans Fat: 0.0 g | Polyunsaturated Fat: 1.5 g | Monounsaturated Fat: 2.5 g | Cholesterol: 49 mg | Sodium: 97 mg | Carbohydrates: 7 g| Fiber: 1 g | Sugars: 2 g |

Protein: 21 g

Pan-Roasted Cod with Pineapple-Cilantro Salsa

Prep time: 10 minutes | Cook time: 15 minutes | Serves 2

- 2 teaspoons avocado oil
- 2 (4-ounce) cod fillets, skin removed
- ½ teaspoon Mediterranean Seasoning Rub Blend
- 1 cup diced pineapple
- ¼ cup finely chopped fresh cilantro
- 2 tablespoons lime juice

1. In a medium skillet, heat the oil over medium to low heat for 3 minutes until the skillet is hot.
2. Coat the cod fillets evenly with the spice blend and place in the pot. Cook for 3 minutes, until ¼ inch of the fillet is opaque and doesn't stick to the pan. It should be easy to flip. Cook on the other side for another minute, until the cod is soft and flaky.
3. In a medium mixing bowl, combine the pineapple, cilantro, and lime juice. Plate the cod on a serving plate and divide the salsa evenly on each fillet.

PER SERVING

Calories: 167 | Total fat: 5g | Saturated fat: 1g | Cholesterol: 55mg | Sodium: 128mg | Potassium: 401mg | Magnesium: 13mg | Carbohydrates: 13g | Sugars: 9g | Fiber: 2g | Protein: 18g | Added sugar: 0g | Vitamin K: 7mcg

Sesame-Orange Salmon

Prep time: 10 minutes | Cook time: 16 minutes |
Serves 4

- Cooking spray
- 4 salmon fillets with skin (about 5 ounces each) or 4 skinless salmon fillets (about 4 ounces each), rinsed and patted dry
- 2 tablespoons fresh orange juice and ½ cup fresh orange juice, divided use
- 3 tablespoons sesame seeds
- 1 tablespoon grated orange zest
- ¼ teaspoon salt-free lemon pepper
- 1 teaspoon soy sauce (lowest sodium available)
- ½ teaspoon toasted sesame oil

1. Preheat the oven to 425°F. Line a 13 × 9 × 2-inch baking pan with aluminum foil. Lightly spray with cooking spray.
2. Place the fish in the pan with the skin side down. Brush the top of the fish with 2 tablespoons orange juice.
3. In a small bowl, stir together the sesame seeds, orange zest, and lemon pepper. Sprinkle over the top of the fish.
4. Bake for 10 to 12 minutes, or until the fish is cooked to the desired doneness. Remove the skin if desired (tongs work well for this).

PER SERVING

Calories: 235 | Total Fat: 10.5 g | Saturated Fat: 2.0 g | Trans Fat: 0.0 g | Polyunsaturated Fat: 3.0 g | Monounsaturated Fat: 3.5 g | Cholesterol: 60 mg | Sodium: 134 mg | Carbohydrates: 5 g| Fiber: 1 g | Sugars: 4 g | Protein: 29 g

Mini Crab Casseroles

Prep time: 10 minutes | Cook time: 28 minutes |
Serves 8

- Cooking spray
- ½ teaspoon canola or corn oil
- 2 tablespoons minced onion
- 2 cups fat-free milk
- 3 tablespoons all-purpose flour
- 1 medium rib of celery, finely chopped, or ¼ teaspoon celery seeds
- 1 2-ounce jar diced pimientos, drained
- 2 tablespoons minced green bell pepper
- 1 tablespoon chopped fresh parsley
- Dash of red hot-pepper sauce
- 2 tablespoons dry sherry
- ¼ cup egg substitute
- 3 cups flaked crabmeat, thawed if frozen or rinsed and drained if canned, bits of shell and cartilage discarded
- ¼ teaspoon pepper, or to taste
- 2 slices whole-grain bread (lowest sodium available), lightly toasted and crumbled

1. Preheat the oven to 350°F. Lightly spray eight ramekins or individual casserole dishes with cooking spray.
2. In a large nonstick skillet, heat the oil over medium-high heat, swirling to coat the bottom. Cook the onion for about 3 minutes, or until soft, stirring frequently.
3. In a medium bowl, whisk together the milk and flour. Stir into the onion. Cook for 3 to 5 minutes, or until thickened, stirring occasionally.
4. Stir in the celery, pimientos, bell pepper, parsley, and hot-pepper sauce. Remove from the heat. Stir in the sherry.
5. Pour the egg substitute into a small bowl. Whisk in a little of the onion mixture.

PER SERVING

Calories: 118 | Total Fat: 1.0 g | Saturated Fat: 0.0 g | Trans Fat: 0.0 g | Polyunsaturated Fat: 0.5 g | Monounsaturated Fat: 0.0 g | Cholesterol: 42 mg | Sodium: 273 mg | Carbohydrates: 10 g| Fiber: 1 g | Sugars: 4 g | Protein: 16 g

Oven-Fried Oysters

Prep time: 10 minutes | Cook time: 8 minutes | Serves 4

- Cooking spray
- ¼ cup low-fat buttermilk
- ½ teaspoon red hot-pepper sauce
- 24 shucked oysters, rinsed and drained
- ½ cup all-purpose flour
- 2 large egg whites, beaten until frothy
- 1 ½ cups crushed cornflakes
- 1 tablespoon salt-free all-purpose seasoning blend
- ⅛ teaspoon cayenne
- ½ cup no-salt-added ketchup
- 1 tablespoon bottled white horseradish, drained
- 2 teaspoons fresh lemon juice
- 1 teaspoon Worcestershire sauce (lowest sodium available)
- 1 medium lemon, cut into 4 wedges

1. Preheat the oven to 400°F. Place a wire cooling rack on a large rimmed baking sheet. Lightly spray the rack and baking sheet with cooking spray.
2. In a medium bowl, whisk together the buttermilk and hot-pepper sauce. Add the oysters, stirring gently to coat. (For deeper flavor and additional tenderness, cover and refrigerate the oysters for up to 30 minutes at this point if desired.)
3. Put the flour in a medium shallow bowl. Put the egg whites in a separate medium shallow bowl. In a third medium shallow bowl, stir together the cornflakes, seasoning blend, and cayenne. Put the bowls and baking sheet in a row, assembly-line fashion.
4. Drain the oysters, discarding the buttermilk mixture. Dip the oysters in the flour, then in the egg whites, and finally in the cornflake mixture, turning to coat at each step and gently shaking off the excess. Using your fingertips, gently press the coating so it adheres to the oysters. Place the oysters on the wire rack.
5. Bake for 7 to 8 minutes, or until the oysters are crisp on the outside and cooked on the inside (slightly firm when pressed with the back of a spoon).
6. Meanwhile, in a small bowl, whisk together the ketchup, horseradish, lemon juice, and Worcestershire sauce. Serve the oysters with the sauce and the lemon wedges.

PER SERVING

Calories: 171 | Total Fat: 1.5 g | Saturated Fat: 0.5 g | Trans Fat: 0.0 g | Polyunsaturated Fat: 0.5 g | Monounsaturated Fat: 0.0 g | Cholesterol: 34 mg | Sodium: 219 mg | Carbohydrates: 32 g| Fiber: 1 g | Sugars: 11 g | Protein: 7 g

Sardines Puttanesca

Prep time: 10 minutes | Cook time: 15 minutes |
Serves 2

- 2 teaspoons avocado oil
- 1 medium yellow onion, diced
- 2 large garlic cloves, minced
- 1 pound medium roma tomatoes, cut into ½-inch pieces
- 7½ ounces no-salt-added canned sardines, in water
- ¼ cup low-sodium kalamata olives, quartered
- ½ teaspoon dried oregano
- ½ cup fresh chopped fresh parsley
- ¼ teaspoon red pepper flakes
- ½ teaspoon freshly ground black pepper

1. In a medium skillet, heat the oil over medium-high heat. Add the onions and garlic and sauté until translucent, about 2 minutes.
2. Add the tomatoes and cover for 5 minutes, until the tomatoes have softened and their juices are exposed.
3. Drain the sardines and, in a small bowl, mash well with a fork.
4. Add the sardines, olives, oregano, parsley, red pepper flakes, and black pepper to the tomato, onion, and garlic mixture. Mix well and cook on medium-low heat, covered, for another 5 minutes. Serve on top of ½ cup of whole wheat pasta or bean pasta, or alongside Whole Wheat Seed Crackers.

PER SERVING

Calories: 278 | Total fat: 15g | Saturated fat: 3g | Cholesterol: 51mg | Sodium: 241mg | Potassium: 1014mg | Magnesium: 65mg | Carbohydrates: 17g | Sugars: 9g | Fiber: 4g | Protein: 22g | Added sugar: 0g | Vitamin K: 266mcg

Grilled Pineapple-Lime Salmon

Prep time: 10 minutes | Cook time: 22 minutes |
Serves 6

- 6 ounces 100% pineapple juice
- ½ cup finely chopped onion
- ½ teaspoon grated lime zest
- 2 tablespoons fresh lime juice
- 1 tablespoon grated peeled gingerroot
- 1 tablespoon soy sauce (lowest sodium available)
- 2 medium garlic cloves, minced
- 1 teaspoon hot chili oil (optional)
- 1 teaspoon canola or corn oil
- 6 salmon steaks or fillets (about 4 ounces each), rinsed and patted dry
- Cooking spray

1. In a large shallow glass dish, stir together the marinade ingredients. Add the fish, turning to coat. Cover and refrigerate for 15 minutes to 1 hour, turning occasionally.
2. Lightly spray the grill rack or a broiler pan and rack with cooking spray. Preheat the grill on medium high or preheat the broiler.
3. Drain the fish, discarding the marinade. Grill or broil about 4 inches from the heat for 5 to 7 minutes on each side, or to the desired doneness.

PER SERVING

Calories: 146 | Total Fat: 5.0 g | Saturated Fat: 1.0 g | Trans Fat: 0.0 g | Polyunsaturated Fat: 1.0 g | Monounsaturated Fat: 1.5 g | Cholesterol: 52 mg | Sodium: 150 mg | Carbohydrates: 0 g| Fiber: 0 g | Sugars: 0 g | Protein: 23 g

Chapter 8

Poultry

Kung Pao Chicken

Prep time: 15 minutes | Cook time: 6 to 7 hours on low | Serves 6

- nonstick cooking spray
- 2 pounds boneless, skinless chicken breast, cut into 1-inch pieces
- 1 (8-ounce) can water chestnuts, drained
- 2 celery stalks, chopped
- 1 red bell pepper chopped
- 1 green bell pepper chopped
- 4 medium carrots, sliced
- ½ cup plus 2 tablespoons water, divided
- ¼ cup low-sodium soy sauce
- ¼ cup balsamic vinegar
- 4 tablespoons sriracha sauce (or to taste)
- 4 garlic cloves, minced
- 2 tablespoons honey (or to taste)
- 1 tablespoon freshly grated ginger
- 1 tablespoon sesame oil
- 2 tablespoons cornstarch
- 2 cups snow peas

1. Spray the inside of a slow cooker with the cooking spray. Add the chicken, water chestnuts, celery, bell peppers, and carrots.
2. In a small bowl, whisk together ½ cup water, the soy sauce, balsamic vinegar, sriracha, garlic, honey, ginger, and sesame oil. Pour this over the chicken and vegetables. Cover and cook on low for 5 to 6 hours.
3. About 20 minutes before serving, whisk together the cornstarch and remaining 2 tablespoons of water until the cornstarch is dissolved. Stir this into the slow cooker along with the snow peas and continue cooking until sauce has thickened, 15 to 20 minutes depending on how hot your slow cooker gets.
4. Serve hot over rice or vegetables noodles garnished with chopped nuts and chopped scallions, if desired.

PER SERVING

Calories: 312 | Total Fat: 8g | Saturated Fat: 3g | Trans Fat: 0g | Polyunsaturated Fat: 1g | Monounsaturated Fat: 3g | Cholesterol: 87mg | Sodium: 587mg | Carbohydrates: 24g | Fiber: 4g | Sugars: 13g | Protein: 36g

Chicken Cordon Bleu

Prep time: 10 minutes | Cook time: 15 minutes | Serves 4

- 4 boneless, skinless chicken breast halves (about 4 ounces each), all visible fat discarded, flattened to ¼-inch thickness
- 2 slices low-fat Swiss cheese (about 2 ounces), halved
- 2 slices lower-sodium, low-fat ham (about 2 ounces), all visible fat discarded
- ½ cup chopped cooked spinach (about 8 to 10 ounces fresh)
- 4 teaspoons chopped fresh chives
- 3 tablespoons whole-wheat flour
- 1 teaspoon dry mustard
- ½ teaspoon paprika
- 2 teaspoons olive oil

1. Arrange the chicken on a work surface. Place half a slice of Swiss and a slice of ham on top of each breast. If the cheese or ham hangs over the edges of the chicken breast, cut it or fold it to fit it on top. Spread 2 tablespoons spinach on top of the ham. Sprinkle each breast with 1 teaspoon of chives. Starting with a short side, roll up jelly-roll style. Secure with wooden toothpicks.
2. In a medium shallow bowl, stir together the flour, mustard, and paprika. Dip the chicken in the flour mixture, turning lightly to coat and gently shaking off any excess. Transfer to a large plate.
3. In a large nonstick skillet, heat the oil over medium-low heat, swirling to coat the bottom. Cook the chicken for about 15 minutes on each side, or until golden brown on the outside and no longer pink in the center. Cook each seam side for about 20 seconds to seal.

PER SERVING

Calories: 228 | Total Fat: 7.0 g | Saturated Fat: 1.5 g | Trans Fat: 0.0 g | Polyunsaturated Fat: 1.0 g | Monounsaturated Fat: 3.0 g | Cholesterol: 84 mg | Sodium: 337 mg | Carbohydrates: 8 g| Fiber: 2 g | Sugars: 1 g | Protein: 33 g

Indonesian Chicken Curry

Prep time: 10 minutes | Cook time: 33 minutes | Serves 4

- ¾ cup uncooked brown rice (jasmine preferred)
- 2 teaspoons canola or corn oil
- 4 boneless, skinless chicken thighs (about 4 ounces each), all visible fat discarded
- 1 cup fat-free, low-sodium chicken broth
- ⅓ cup lite coconut milk
- 1 stalk lemongrass (use the bottom 8 inches of the stalk), cut in half lengthwise and slightly pounded with a meat mallet, or 1 teaspoon lemongrass paste
- 1 cinnamon stick (about 3 inches long)
- 2 medium garlic cloves, minced
- 2 medium kaffir lime leaves or 1 teaspoon grated lime zest
- 1 teaspoon minced peeled gingerroot
- ¼ teaspoon salt
- ⅛ teaspoon pepper

1. Prepare the rice using the package directions, omitting the salt and margarine.
2. In a large skillet, heat the oil over medium-high heat, swirling to coat the bottom. Cook the chicken for 2 to 3 minutes on each side, or until browned. Stir in the remaining ingredients.

PER SERVING

Calories: 302 | Total Fat: 9.0 g | Saturated Fat: 2.0 g | Trans Fat: 0.0 g | Polyunsaturated Fat: 2.0 g | Monounsaturated Fat: 3.5 g | Cholesterol: 108 mg | Sodium: 263 mg | Carbohydrates: 28 g| Fiber: 1 g | Sugars: 1 g | Protein: 25 g

Szechuan Orange Chicken

Prep time: 10 minutes | Cook time: 11 minutes | Serves 4

- Cooking spray
- 1 teaspoon garlic powder
- 1 teaspoon onion powder
- 1 teaspoon ground ginger and 2 teaspoons ground ginger, divided use
- ½ teaspoon crushed red pepper flakes and ½ teaspoon crushed red pepper flakes, divided use
- 1 pound chicken breast tenders, all visible fat discarded, cut into 1-inch cubes
- 1 teaspoon plain rice vinegar
- ¼ cup egg substitute
- 1 cup panko (Japanese-style bread crumbs)
- ¼ cup plus 2 tablespoons frozen 100% orange juice concentrate, thawed
- ¼ cup plus 2 tablespoons water
- 1 tablespoon plus 1 teaspoon honey
- 2 teaspoons soy sauce (lowest sodium available)
- 2 medium garlic cloves, finely chopped
- 1 teaspoon toasted sesame oil

1. Preheat the broiler. Line a baking sheet with aluminum foil. Lightly spray with cooking spray.
2. In a medium bowl, stir together the garlic powder, onion powder, 1 teaspoon ginger, and ½ teaspoon red pepper flakes. Add the chicken, stirring to coat.
3. Drizzle with the vinegar, stirring to coat. Let stand for 5 minutes.
4. Meanwhile, pour the egg substitute into a shallow dish. Put the panko in a separate shallow dish. Set the dishes and baking sheet in a row, assembly-line fashion. Working in batches, dip the chicken cubes in the egg substitute, then in the panko, turning to coat at each step, and gently shaking off any excess. Place the chicken on the baking sheet in a single layer, arranging so the cubes don't touch. Lightly spray the top and sides of the chicken with cooking spray.
5. Broil about 6 inches from the heat for 8 minutes, or until the chicken is no longer pink in the center and the coating is golden brown and crisp.
6. Meanwhile, in a small microwaveable bowl, whisk together the orange juice concentrate, water, honey, soy sauce, garlic, and the remaining 2 teaspoons ginger. Microwave, covered, on 100 percent power (high) for 3 minutes, or until hot and bubbly.
7. Stir in the sesame oil and the remaining ½ teaspoon red pepper flakes. Drizzle over the chicken.

PER SERVING

Calories: 274 | Total Fat: 4.0 g | Saturated Fat: 1.0 g | Trans Fat: 0.0 g | Polyunsaturated Fat: 1.0 g | Monounsaturated Fat: 1.5 g | Cholesterol: 73 mg | Sodium: 255 mg | Carbohydrates: 30 g| Fiber: 1 g | Sugars: 16 g | Protein: 28 g

Salsa Verde Chicken

Prep time: 10 minutes | Cook time: 5 to 6 hours on low | Serves 6

- nonstick cooking spray
- 2 pounds boneless, skinless chicken breasts
- 2 cups salsa verde
- 1 (14.5-ounce) can no-salt-added fire-roasted tomatoes
- 1 (4-ounce) can green chiles
- 1 bell pepper (any color), chopped
- 2 teaspoons ground cumin
- 1 teaspoon dried oregano
- freshly ground black pepper
- optional toppings: chopped fresh cilantro, avocado slices, lime wedges, lettuce leaves

1. Spray the inside of a 6-quart slow cooker with the cooking spray. Place the chicken in the bottom of the slow cooker. Add the salsa verde, tomatoes, chiles, bell pepper, cumin, oregano, and black pepper, and stir to combine. Cover and cook on low for 5 to 6 hours.
2. Remove the chicken and shred it using two forks. Stir the shredded chicken back into the slow cooker and taste to adjust seasonings.
3. Serve hot, with toppings such as chopped fresh cilantro, avocado slices, or lime wedges, if desired.

PER SERVING

Calories: 257 | Total Fat: 5g | Saturated Fat: 2g | Trans Fat: 0g | Polyunsaturated Fat: 1g | Monounsaturated Fat: 2g | Cholesterol: 87mg | Sodium: 646mg | Carbohydrates: 14g | Fiber: 4g | Sugars: 3g | Protein: 34g

Turkey Rolls with Garden Pesto

Prep time: 10 minutes | Cook time: 45 minutes | Serves 4

- Cooking spray
- Pesto
- ½ cup tightly packed fresh basil
- 1 small tomato, peeled, seeded, and coarsely chopped
- 1 tablespoon pine nuts, dry-roasted
- 1 large garlic clove, minced
- 2 tablespoons shredded or grated Parmesan cheese
- 2 8-ounce turkey tenderloins, all visible fat discarded, halved lengthwise
- 1 tablespoon honey
- 1 tablespoon soy sauce (lowest sodium available)

1. Preheat the oven to 350°F. Lightly spray an 8-inch square baking dish with cooking spray.
2. In a food processor or blender, process the pesto ingredients except the Parmesan until nearly smooth. Stir in the Parmesan.
3. Spread 1 rounded tablespoon pesto mixture on a piece of turkey. Starting with a short side, roll up jelly-roll style. Secure with wooden toothpicks. Repeat with the remaining turkey and pesto mixture. Place the turkey rolls with the seam side down in the pan. Set aside any remaining pesto.
4. In a small bowl, whisk together the honey and soy sauce. Brush on the turkey rolls.
5. Bake for 40 to 45 minutes, or until the turkey is no longer pink in the center. Top the turkey rolls with the remaining pesto.

PER SERVING

Calories: 166 | Total Fat: 2.5 g | Saturated Fat: 1.0 g | Trans Fat: 0.0 g | Polyunsaturated Fat: 0.5 g | Monounsaturated Fat: 0.5 g | Cholesterol: 76 mg | Sodium: 188 mg | Carbohydrates: 7 g| Fiber: 1 g | Sugars: 6 g | Protein: 29 g

Chapter 9

Meats

Simple Sauerbraten

Prep time: 10 minutes | Cook time: 40 minutes | Serves 8

- Cooking spray
- Pepper to taste (freshly ground preferred)
- 3 pounds boneless lean chuck shoulder roast, all visible fat discarded
- 1 cup white wine vinegar
- 1 cup water
- 1 medium onion, sliced
- 2 medium dried bay leaves
- 16 low-fat gingersnaps, crushed to fine crumbs

1. Preheat the oven to 475°F. Lightly spray a Dutch oven with cooking spray.
2. Sprinkle the pepper over the roast. Transfer to the Dutch oven. Roast for 8 to 10 minutes, or until browned, turning once halfway through. Remove from the oven.
3. Pour the vinegar and water over the beef. Arrange the onion slices on the beef. Put the bay leaves in the pot liquid.
4. Reduce the heat to 350°F. Roast, covered, for 1½ hours. Remove from the oven.
5. Sprinkle the gingersnap crumbs over the beef and gravy. Roast, covered, for 30 minutes, or to the desired doneness. Add water as needed to thin the gravy. Transfer the beef to a cutting board. Very thinly slice the beef diagonally across the grain. Discard the bay leaves. Serve with the gravy.

PER SERVING

Calories: 263 | Total Fat: 9.0 g | Saturated Fat: 3.0 g | Trans Fat: 0.0 g | Polyunsaturated Fat: 0.5 g | Monounsaturated Fat: 4.0 g | Cholesterol: 98 mg | Sodium: 114 mg | Carbohydrates: 13 g| Fiber: 0 g | Sugars: 6 g | Protein: 32 g

Braised Sirloin Tips

Prep time: 10 minutes | Cook time: 1 hour 46 minutes | Serves 8

- ¼ teaspoon pepper
- 2 pounds sirloin tip, all visible fat discarded, cut into 1-inch cubes
- 1 small to medium onion, finely chopped
- 2 medium garlic cloves, minced
- 1¼ cups fat-free, low-sodium beef broth
- ⅓ cup dry red wine (regular or nonalcoholic)
- 1 tablespoon soy sauce (lowest sodium available)
- 2 tablespoons cornstarch
- ¼ cup cold water
- ¼ cup chopped fresh parsley

1. Sprinkle the pepper over the beef.
2. In a large, heavy nonstick skillet, cook the beef over medium-high heat for 8 to 10 minutes, or until well browned on all sides, stirring frequently.
3. Stir in the onion and garlic. Cook for 3 minutes, or until the onion is soft, stirring frequently.
4. Stir in the broth, wine, and soy sauce. Bring to a boil. Reduce the heat and simmer, covered, for 1 hour 30 minutes, or until the beef is tender. Transfer the beef to a platter.
5. Put the cornstarch in a small bowl. Add the water, whisking to dissolve. Slowly pour into the skillet, stirring constantly. Increase the heat to medium high.Serve with the beef. Sprinkle with the parsley.

PER SERVING

Calories: 162 | Total Fat: 3.0 g | Saturated Fat: 1.0 g | Trans Fat: 0.0 g | Polyunsaturated Fat: 0.5 g | Monounsaturated Fat: 1.5 g | Cholesterol: 58 mg | Sodium: 124 mg | Carbohydrates: 4 g| Fiber: 1 g | Sugars: 2 g | Protein: 26 g

Pork Roulades

Prep time: 10 minutes | Cook time: 54 minutes | Serves 6

- Cooking spray
- 2 teaspoons canola or corn oil and 1 tablespoon canola or corn oil, divided use
- 8 ounces button mushrooms
- 1 tablespoon chopped onion
- 3 slices whole-grain bread (lowest sodium available), torn into small pieces
- 2 medium ribs of celery, chopped
- ¼ cup chopped walnuts
- 1 teaspoon chopped fresh parsley
- ½ teaspoon dried thyme, crumbled
- ¼ teaspoon salt
- Pepper (freshly ground preferred)
- 2 1-pound pork tenderloins, all visible fat discarded, cut into 6 3 × 4-inch rectangles, then flattened to ¼-inch thickness

Sauce

2 tablespoons all-purpose flour
½ cup fat-free, low-sodium beef broth
1 tablespoon canola or corn oil
Pepper to taste (freshly ground preferred)

1. Preheat the oven to 350°F. Lightly spray a Dutch oven with cooking spray. Set aside.
2. In a medium skillet, heat 2 teaspoons oil over medium-high heat, swirling to coat the bottom. Cook the mushrooms and onion for 4 minutes, or until the onion is soft and beginning to brown, stirring frequently.
3. In a large bowl, stir together the bread, celery, walnuts, parsley, thyme, salt, and pepper. Stir in the mushroom mixture.
4. Divide the filling into 6 portions. Place each portion on a piece of pork. Roll the pork around the filling to form a cylinder. Secure with wooden toothpicks.
5. In the same skillet, still over medium-high heat, heat 1 tablespoon oil, swirling to coat the bottom. Cook the roulades for 5 minutes, turning to brown on all sides. Transfer the roulades to the Dutch oven. Bake, covered, for 1½ hours.
6. About 30 minutes before the end of the baking time, put the flour in a medium saucepan. Add the broth and the remaining 1 tablespoon oil, whisking to dissolve. Whisk in the pepper. Heat over medium heat, whisking frequently.
7. About 15 minutes before the end of the baking time, uncover the Dutch oven. Spoon half the sauce over the roulades as a glaze. Return to the oven.
8. Serve the roulades with the remaining sauce.

PER SERVING

Calories: 298 | Total Fat: 14.0 g | Saturated Fat: 2.5 g | Trans Fat: 0.0 g | Polyunsaturated Fat: 4.0 g | Monounsaturated Fat: 6.0 g | Cholesterol: 80 mg | Sodium: 224 mg | Carbohydrates: 10 g| Fiber: 2 g | Sugars: 2 g | Protein: 33 g

Sliced Pork Loin For Sandwiches

Prep time: 10 minutes | Cook time: 30 minutes |
Serves 4

- 1 teaspoon onion powder
- ½ teaspoon garlic powder
- ½ teaspoon dried thyme
- ¼ teaspoon kosher salt
- ¼ teaspoon freshly ground black pepper
- 1 (1-pound) boneless pork tenderloin roast
- 1 tablespoon canola or sunflower oil

1. Preheat the oven to 425°F.
2. Mix the onion powder, garlic powder, thyme, salt, and pepper in a small bowl. Trim the tenderloin of any silverskin, and pat dry. Rub all over with the seasoning.
3. Heat the oil in a large, oven-safe skillet over medium-high heat. (If you don't have an oven-safe skillet, use a regular skillet and place an aluminum foil–lined roasting pan in the oven to heat up.) When the skillet is very hot, sear the pork for 2 minutes on each side. Transfer the skillet to the oven (or transfer the steak to the roasting pan).
4. Cook until the internal temperature reaches 145°F, about 15 minutes. Tent lightly with foil for at least 5 minutes before slicing.

PER SERVING

Calories: 158 | Total Fat: 6g | Saturated Fat: 1g | Cholesterol: 74mg | Sodium: 181mg | Carbohydrates: 1g | Fiber: 0g | Added Sugars: 0g | Protein: 24g | Potassium: 464mg | Vitamin K: 5mcg

Philadelphia-Style Cheese Steak Wrap

Prep time: 10 minutes | Cook time: 15 minutes |
Serves 6

- 1 tablespoon balsamic vinegar or red wine vinegar
- 2 teaspoons Worcestershire sauce (lowest sodium available)
- 1 teaspoon sugar
- 1 teaspoon dried oregano, crumbled
- 1 teaspoon olive oil
- 2 medium garlic cloves, minced
- ¼ teaspoon pepper
- 12 ounces eye-of-round roast, all visible fat discarded, cut diagonally across the grain into ⅛-inch slices
- 1 small onion, thinly sliced
- 1 medium green bell pepper, thinly sliced
- 6 6-inch whole-wheat tortillas (lowest sodium available)
- 2 1-ounce slices fat-free sharp Cheddar cheese, each cut into thirds

1. In a medium glass dish, stir together the marinade ingredients until the sugar is dissolved. Add the beef, turning to coat. Cover and refrigerate for 10 minutes to 8 hours, turning occasionally.
2. Preheat the oven to 350°F.
3. Heat a nonstick griddle or large nonstick skillet over medium-high heat. Drain the beef, discarding the marinade. Cook for 3 to 5 minutes, or until no longer pink, stirring occasionally. Transfer to a bowl. Cover to keep warm.
4. Wipe the griddle with paper towels. Cook the onion and bell pepper for about 5 minutes, or until soft, stirring occasionally.

PER SERVING

Calories: 173 | Total Fat: 2.5 g | Saturated Fat: 0.5 g | Trans Fat: 0.0 g | Polyunsaturated Fat: 0.5 g | Monounsaturated Fat: 1.5 g | Cholesterol: 29 mg | Sodium: 334 mg | Carbohydrates: 18 g| Fiber: 3 g | Sugars: 4 g | Protein: 19 g

Caribbean Kebabs

**Prep time: 10 minutes | Cook time: 18 minutes |
Serves 4**

- 1 20-ounce can pineapple chunks in their own juice, drained, ¼ cup juice reserved
- 1 teaspoon grated lemon zest
- 2 tablespoons fresh lemon juice
- 1 teaspoon light molasses
- ⅛ teaspoon pepper
- 1 pound boneless sirloin steak, all visible fat discarded, cut into 16 1-inch cubes
- 1 medium mango, cut into 8 cubes, or 1 medium star fruit (carambola), cut crosswise into 8 slices, seeds discarded
- ⅔ cup uncooked instant brown rice
- Cooking spray
- 1 medium zucchini, cut into 8 slices
- 12 pearl onions, thawed if frozen
- 1 medium red bell pepper, cut into 12 1-inch squares
- 1 tablespoon plus 1 teaspoon shredded unsweetened coconut, toasted

1. Set the pineapple chunks aside. Pour the reserved pineapple juice into a shallow glass bowl or casserole dish. Stir the lemon zest, lemon juice, molasses, and pepper into the pineapple juice. Add the beef cubes, turning to coat. Cover and refrigerate for 2 to 12 hours, stirring occasionally. Drain the beef, discarding the marinade.
2. Soak four 10-inch wooden skewers for at least 10 minutes in cold water to keep them from charring (these will be for skewering the beef), or use metal skewers. On four unsoaked 10-inch wooden or metal skewers, thread the pineapple chunks and mango cubes so they're evenly distributed among the skewers. Cover and refrigerate.
3. Prepare the rice using the package directions, omitting the salt and margarine. Set aside.
4. Meanwhile, preheat the broiler. Lightly spray a broiler pan with cooking spray. For each kebab, thread each skewer with 4 beef cubes, 2 zucchini slices, 3 onions, and 3 bell pepper squares. Transfer the beef skewers to the broiler pan.
5. Broil 4 to 6 inches from the heat for 3 to 4 minutes on each side, or until the desired doneness. You can also grill these skewers over medium-high heat for 3 to 4 minutes on each side, or until the desired doneness.
6. Spoon the rice down the center of each plate. Place a beef skewer on one side of the plate and a chilled fruit skewer on the other. Sprinkle the coconut over the rice.

PER SERVING

Calories: 361 | Total Fat: 7.0 g | Saturated Fat: 3.0 g | Trans Fat: 0.0 g | Polyunsaturated Fat: 0.5 g | Monounsaturated Fat: 2.5 g | Cholesterol: 60 mg | Sodium: 79 mg | Carbohydrates: 47 g| Fiber: 5 g | Sugars: 31 g | Protein: 29 g

Chapter 10

Vegetables and Side Dishes

Scalloped Squash

Prep time: 10 minutes | Cook time: 13 minutes | Serves 6

- 1 teaspoon light tub margarine
- 1 large onion, finely chopped
- 1½ pounds yellow summer squash, sliced
- ⅔ cup fat-free, low-sodium chicken broth
- 1 teaspoon dried basil, crumbled
- 1 teaspoon dried thyme, crumbled
- 1 teaspoon dried marjoram, crumbled
- ¼ teaspoon salt
- 1 ¾ cups unseasoned croutons (lowest sodium available), crushed
- ¼ cup chopped fresh chives

1. In a large saucepan, melt the margarine over medium-high heat, swirling to coat the bottom. Cook the onion for about 3 minutes, or until soft, stirring frequently.
2. Stir in the squash, broth, basil, thyme, marjoram, and salt. Reduce the heat to medium. Cook, covered, for 10 minutes, or until the squash is tender.
3. Stir in the croutons. If the mixture is too dry, stir in a small amount of hot water. Stir in the chives.

PER SERVING

Calories: 76 | Total Fat: 0.5 g | Saturated Fat: 0.0 g | Trans Fat: 0.0 g | Polyunsaturated Fat: 0.0 g | Monounsaturated Fat: 0.0 g | Cholesterol: 0 mg | Sodium: 194 mg | Carbohydrates: 16 g| Fiber: 2 g | Sugars: 5 g | Protein: 3 g

Spicy Spinach and Almond Stir-Fry

Prep time: 10 minutes | Cook time: 10 minutes | Serves 4

- 3 teaspoons olive oil, divided 2 eggs, beaten
- 2 garlic cloves, minced
- ¾ cup chopped scallions
- 1 cup thinly sliced Brussels sprouts
- 4 cups baby spinach
- ¼ cup sliced almonds
- 2 cups cooked and chilled brown rice
- 2 teaspoons reduced-sodium tamari or soy sauce
- 2 teaspoons sriracha
- 1 lime, halved
- ¼ cup chopped fresh cilantro, for garnish

1. Heat a large (12-inch or wider) wok or nonstick frying pan over medium-high heat. Once the pan is hot enough that a drop of water sizzles on contact, add 1 teaspoon of olive oil. Pour in the eggs and cook, stirring occasionally, until the eggs are scrambled and lightly set, about 3 minutes. Transfer the eggs to a medium bowl.
2. Add 1 teaspoon of olive oil to the pan and add the garlic, scallions, and Brussels sprouts. Cook, stirring frequently, for 30 seconds, or until fragrant. Add the spinach and continue to cook, stirring frequently, for about 2 minutes, or until the spinach is wilted and tender. Transfer the mixture to the bowl of eggs.
3. Add the almonds to the pan and cook, stirring frequently, for about 1 minute, or until they are crisp and lightly browned. Add the remaining 1 teaspoon of olive oil and the rice to the pan and cook, stirring occasionally, for about 3 minutes until the rice is hot.
4. Pour the contents of the bowl back into the pan. Add the tamari, sriracha, and juice from half a lime. Stir to combine and remove from the heat.

PER SERVING

Calories: 587 | Fats: 20g | Protein: 20g | Cholesterol: 164mg | Carbohydrates: 86g | Fiber: 9g | Sodium: 557mg

Rosemary Kale with Almonds

Prep time: 10 minutes | Cook time: 10 minutes | Serves 6

- 2 pounds fresh kale, ribs and any tough stems discarded, coarsely chopped, or 20 ounces frozen leaf kale, thawed and drained
- ½ cup fat-free, low-sodium vegetable broth
- 2 tablespoons chopped red onion
- ½ teaspoon sugar
- 1 teaspoon dried rosemary, crushed
- ¼ teaspoon salt
- Pepper to taste (freshly ground preferred)
- 1 teaspoon olive oil
- 1 teaspoon toasted sesame oil
- ¼ cup sliced almonds, dry-roasted

1. In a large saucepan, stir together the kale, broth, onion, sugar, and rosemary. Cook, covered, over medium-high heat for 10 minutes, or until the kale is tender, stirring occasionally. Remove from the heat.
2. Stir in the salt and pepper.
3. Just before serving, stir in the oils. Sprinkle with the almonds.

PER SERVING

Calories: 113 | Total Fat: 5.0 g | Saturated Fat: 0.5 g | Trans Fat: 0.0 g | Polyunsaturated Fat: 1.5 g | Monounsaturated Fat: 2.0 g | Cholesterol: 0 mg | Sodium: 156 mg | Carbohydrates: 15 g| Fiber: 4 g | Sugars: 1 g | Protein: 7 g

Southern-Style Greens

Prep time: 10 minutes | Cook time: 14 minutes | Serves 4

- 6 ounces collard greens, tough stems discarded, leaves coarsely chopped
- 6 ounces kale, tough stems discarded, leaves coarsely chopped
- 4 ounces Swiss chard, tough stems discarded, leaves coarsely chopped
- 1 teaspoon canola or corn oil
- 2 slices turkey bacon, chopped
- ⅓ cup chopped onion
- 2 tablespoons balsamic vinegar
- 1 teaspoon pure maple syrup
- 2 tablespoons chopped pecans, dry-roasted

1. Pour 3 to 3 ½ quarts of water into a large stockpot. Bring to a boil over high heat. Boil the collard greens for 5 minutes. Add the chard. Boil for 2 to 3 minutes, or until the greens are tender. Transfer to a colander. Run under very cold water. Drain well. Gently squeeze out the excess water. Pat the greens dry with paper towels.
2. In a large nonstick skillet, heat the oil over medium heat, swirling to coat the bottom. Cook the bacon and onion for 3 to 4 minutes, or until the bacon is lightly browned, stirring frequently. Stir in the greens. Cook for 1 to 2 minutes, or until hot. Add the vinegar and maple syrup, stirring until the greens are coated. Just before serving, sprinkle with the pecans.

PER SERVING

Calories: 109 | Total Fat: 5.5 g | Saturated Fat: 1.0 g | Trans Fat: 0.0 g | Polyunsaturated Fat: 1.5 g | Monounsaturated Fat: 3.0 g | Cholesterol: 5 mg | Sodium: 247 mg | Carbohydrates: 12 g| Fiber: 3 g | Sugars: 4 g | Protein: 5 g

Gingered Acorn Squash

Prep time: 10 minutes | Cook time: 47 minutes |
Serves 4

- Cooking spray
- 2 medium acorn squash (about ¾ pound each), halved lengthwise, seeds and strings discarded
- 1 8-ounce can pineapple tidbits in their own juice, drained
- 3 tablespoons raisins (optional)
- 2 tablespoons light brown sugar
- 1 tablespoon light tub margarine, melted
- 1 teaspoon grated peeled gingerroot

1. Preheat the oven to 400°F. Lightly spray a 13 × 9 × 2-inch baking dish with cooking spray.
2. Put the squash halves with the cut side up in the baking dish.
3. In a small bowl, stir together the remaining ingredients. Spoon the mixture into the cavity of each squash. Carefully pour a small amount of water around, but not over, the squash.
4. Bake, covered, for 45 minutes to 1 hour, or until the squash is tender when pierced with the tip of a sharp knife.

PER SERVING

Calories: 107 | Total Fat: 1.5 g | Saturated Fat: 0.0 g | Trans Fat: 0.0 g | Polyunsaturated Fat: 0.5 g | Monounsaturated Fat: 0.5 g | Cholesterol: 0 mg | Sodium: 32 mg | Carbohydrates: 26 g| Fiber: 2 g | Sugars: 15 g | Protein: 1 g

Savory Cheesy Rosemary Oatmeal

Prep time: 5 minutes | Cook time: 15 minutes |
Serves 4

- 1 cup gluten-free rolled oats
- 1 cup water

- 1 cup unsweetened almond milk or nonfat milk
- ⅔ cup frozen green peas
- 1 teaspoon olive oil
- ½ cup sliced button mushrooms
- 1 cup firmly packed chopped baby spinach
- 1 cup chopped tomato
- 1 tablespoon fresh rosemary
- ½ cup part-skim ricotta cheese
- Salt
- Freshly ground black pepper

1. In a medium pot over medium heat, bring the oats, water, and almond milk to a boil, stirring occasionally. Add the peas, decrease the heat to medium low, and cook for 1 to 2 minutes, stirring often to prevent sticking and burning. Decrease the heat to low.
2. Meanwhile, heat the olive oil in a medium skillet over medium heat. Add the mushrooms and spinach and sauté for 3 to 4 minutes, or until the mushrooms start to release their liquid and the spinach is slightly wilted.
3. Add the tomato and rosemary to the mushroom-spinach mixture and cook for 3 minutes.
4. Add the ricotta to the oats and stir to combine. Transfer the vegetable mixture to the oat mixture and stir until well incorporated. Season with salt and pepper and serve warm.

PER SERVING

Calories: 393 | Fats: 11g | Protein: 21g | Cholesterol: 22mg | Carbohydrates: 50g | Fiber: 9g | Sodium: 243mg

Mexican Fried Rice

Prep time: 10 minutes | Cook time: 33 minutes | Serves 6

- 1 teaspoon canola or corn oil
- 1 cup uncooked long-grain rice
- 2 cups fat-free, low-sodium chicken broth
- ⅔ cup canned chopped green chiles, drained
- 4 to 5 medium green onions, thinly sliced
- ½ cup diced tomatoes
- 1 medium garlic clove, minced

1. In a large, heavy nonstick skillet, heat the oil over medium-high heat, swirling to coat the bottom. Cook the rice for 2 to 3 minutes, or until golden brown, stirring constantly.
2. Stir in the remaining ingredients. Reduce the heat and simmer, covered, for 30 minutes, or until the rice is tender and the liquid is absorbed. Fluff with a fork.

PER SERVING

Calories: 149 | Total Fat: 1.0 g | Saturated Fat: 0.0 g | Trans Fat: 0.0 g | Polyunsaturated Fat: 0.5 g | Monounsaturated Fat: 0.5 g | Cholesterol: 0 mg | Sodium: 112 mg | Carbohydrates: 30 g| Fiber: 2 g | Sugars: 1 g | Protein: 3 g

Tofu Vegetable Stir-Fry

Prep time: 15 minutes | Cook time: 45 minutes | Serves 4

For The Sauce
- 2 teaspoons low-sodium soy sauce
- 3 to 4 tablespoons water
- 1 tablespoon peeled and grated fresh ginger
- 1 tablespoon honey
- 1 tablespoon rice wine vinegar
- 1 tablespoon cornstarch

For The Stir-Fry
- 1 (14-ounce) package firm or extra-firm tofu, drained for 15 minutes
- 1 tablespoon olive oil
- 1 cup diced red bell pepper
- 1 cup broccoli florets
- 1 cup snow peas

To Make The Sauce
1. In a small mixing bowl, whisk together all the sauce ingredients and set it aside.

To Make The Stir-Fry
1. Preheat the oven to 400°F and line a baking sheet with parchment paper, or lightly grease the baking sheet.
2. Chop the tofu into 1-inch cubes and spread them on the prepared baking sheet. Bake for 25 to 35 minutes, flipping halfway through to ensure even cooking.
3. Once the tofu is golden brown and a bit firm, remove it from the oven and set it aside to dry while you prepare the vegetables.
4. Heat the olive oil in a large skillet over medium-high heat. Add the bell pepper, broccoli, and snow peas and cook, stirring often, for 5 to 7 minutes. Give the sauce a quick stir and when the vegetables have some color and are softened, add the sauce to the pan and stir. It should bubble and thicken.
5. Add the tofu and stir to coat. Cook the mixture for 3 to 5 minutes, stirring often. When the veggies are cooked to your liking, remove from the heat and serve.

PER SERVING

Calories: 331 | Fats: 16g | Protein: 21g | Cholesterol: 0mg | Carbohydrates: 31g | Fiber: 7g | Sodium: 344mg

Chapter 11

Desserts

Apple-Cherry Drops

Prep time: 10 minutes | Cook time: 25 minutes | Serves 4

- Cooking spray
- 2 ½ cups all-purpose flour
- 1 teaspoon baking powder
- 1 teaspoon baking soda
- 1 teaspoon ground cinnamon
- ¼ teaspoon ground nutmeg
- ¼ teaspoon salt
- 1 cup sugar
- ½ cup light tub margarine
- ¼ cup firmly packed light brown sugar
- 1 teaspoon vanilla extract
- ½ teaspoon almond extract
- ¼ cup egg substitute
- ¼ cup unsweetened applesauce
- 1 cup shredded peeled apple (about 1 large; Granny Smith, Gala, or Fuji preferred)
- ½ cup unsweetened dried cherries, coarsely chopped

1. Preheat the oven to 350°F. Lightly spray two baking sheets with cooking spray.
2. In a medium bowl, stir together the flour, baking powder, baking soda, cinnamon, nutmeg, and salt.
3. In a large bowl, using an electric mixer on medium speed, beat the sugar, margarine, brown sugar, and vanilla and almond extracts for 3 minutes.
4. Add the egg substitute and applesauce. Beat for 20 to 30 seconds, or until combined.
5. Gradually add the flour mixture, beating on low speed for 1 minute, or until no flour is visible.
6. Stir in the apple and cherries. Using about half the dough, drop by heaping teaspoonfuls about 2 inches apart on the baking sheets to make 32 cookies.
7. Bake for 10 to 12 minutes, or until light brown. Transfer the baking sheets to cooling racks. Let the cookies partially cool on the baking sheets, about 10 minutes. Transfer the cookies to the cooling racks. Repeat with the remaining batter.

PER SERVING

Calories: 88 | Total Fat: 1.0 g | Saturated Fat: 0.0 g | Trans Fat: 0.0 g | Polyunsaturated Fat: 0.5 g | Monounsaturated Fat: 0.5 g | Cholesterol: 0 mg | Sodium: 97 mg | Carbohydrates: 18 g| Fiber: 1 g | Sugars: 10 g | Protein: 1 g

Spiced Baked Apples

Prep time: 15 minutes | Cook time: 4 to 5 hours on low | Serves 6

- 6 apples
- 1 cup rolled oats
- ⅓ cup chopped almonds
- 2 tablespoons brown sugar
- 2 teaspoons pumpkin pie spice
- ½ cup apple juice
- 2 tablespoons extra-virgin olive oil

1. Core the apples using an apple corer or sharp knife. Chop off the top of the apple along with its stem so that the top of the apple is even.
2. In a medium bowl, combine the oats, almonds, brown sugar, and pumpkin pie spice.
3. Stuff the apple cavities with the oat mixture, pressing the mixture down firmly to pack it in. Top off the apples with any remaining oat mixture.

PER SERVING

Calories: 240 | Total Fat: 8g | Saturated Fat: 1g | Trans Fat: 0g | Polyunsaturated Fat: 2g | Monounsaturated Fat: 6g | Cholesterol: 0mg | Sodium: 4mg | Carbohydrates: 42g | Fiber: 7g | Sugars: 24g | Protein: 3g

Chocolate-Mint Pudding

Prep time: 10 minutes | Cook time: 25 minutes | Serves 4

- 2 cups fat-free milk
- ½ cup tightly packed sprigs of fresh mint and 4 sprigs of fresh mint, divided use
- ¼ cup egg substitute
- 2 tablespoons plus 2 teaspoons sugar
- 2 tablespoons cornstarch
- 2 tablespoons unsweetened dark cocoa powder
- ¼ teaspoon mint extract

1. In a heavy, medium saucepan, bring the milk to a boil over medium-high heat. Remove from the heat. Stir in the ½ cup of mint sprigs. Let stand, covered, for 15 minutes.
2. Strain the milk through a fine-mesh sieve into a medium bowl. Pour the strained milk back into the pan.
3. Whisk in the egg substitute, sugar, cornstarch, and cocoa powder until the sugar and cornstarch are dissolved. Cook, still over medium-high heat, for 8 to 10 minutes, or until the mixture comes to a full boil and begins to thicken, whisking constantly. Remove from the heat. Stir in the mint extract.
4. Spoon the pudding into dessert dishes. Garnish with the remaining 4 sprigs of mint.

PER SERVING

Calories: 109 | Total Fat: 0.5 g | Saturated Fat: 0.0 g | Trans Fat: 0.0 g | Polyunsaturated Fat: 0.0 g | Monounsaturated Fat: 0.0 g | Cholesterol: 3 mg | Sodium: 83 mg | Carbohydrates: 20 g| Fiber: 1 g | Sugars: 15 g | Protein: 6 g

Peanut Butter Cookies

Prep time: 10 minutes | Cook time: 15 minutes | Serves 4

- Cooking spray
- ¼ cup light tub margarine, softened
- ¾ cup light brown sugar
- ½ cup sugar
- ⅓ cup low-sodium peanut butter
- 1 large egg
- ¼ cup unsweetened applesauce
- ½ teaspoon baking soda
- 2 ½ cups all-purpose flour
- 1 teaspoon vanilla extract

1. Preheat the oven to 350°F. Lightly spray two large baking sheets with cooking spray.
2. In a large mixing bowl, using an electric mixer on medium speed, cream the margarine. Gradually add both sugars, beating after each addition, until the mixture is creamy. Add the peanut butter, egg, applesauce, and baking soda. Beat well. Gradually add the flour to the batter, beating after each addition. Stir in the vanilla.
3. Roll the dough into 60 balls about the size of a pecan or the bowl of a measuring teaspoon. Transfer to the baking sheets. Flatten the balls slightly using the back of a wet fork.
4. Bake for 12 to 15 minutes, or until the cookies are light brown.

PER SERVING

Calories: 98 | Total Fat: 2.5 g | Saturated Fat: 0.5 g | Trans Fat: 0.0 g | Polyunsaturated Fat: 0.5 g | Monounsaturated Fat: 1.0 g | Cholesterol: 6 mg | Sodium: 43 mg | Carbohydrates: 18 g| Fiber: 1 g | Sugars: 9 g | Protein: 2 g

Spiced Skillet Bananas

Prep time: 10 minutes | Cook time: 3 minutes | Serves 4

- 1 tablespoon light tub margarine
- 2 tablespoons dark brown sugar
- ¼ teaspoon ground cinnamon
- ¼ teaspoon ground nutmeg
- 2 cups sliced bananas (about 3 medium bananas)
- ¼ cup chopped pecans, dry-roasted

1. In a large nonstick skillet over medium-high heat, melt the margarine, swirling to coat the bottom. Add the brown sugar, cinnamon, and nutmeg, stirring until the mixture is bubbly and the brown sugar is dissolved.
2. Add the bananas, stirring gently to coat. Cook for 3 minutes, or until just softened and beginning to glaze and turn golden. Don't overcook, or the bananas will break down. Remove from the heat.
3. Just before serving, sprinkle with the pecans. Serve immediately.

PER SERVING

Calories: 151 | Total Fat: 6.5 g | Saturated Fat: 0.5 g | Trans Fat: 0.0 g | Polyunsaturated Fat: 2.0 g | Monounsaturated Fat: 3.5 g | Cholesterol: 0 mg | Sodium: 25 mg | Carbohydrates: 25 g| Fiber: 3 g | Sugars: 16 g | Protein: 2 g

Chocolate Mousse

Prep time: 5 minutes | Cook time: 10 minutes | Serves 6

- 1 (3.5-ounce) bar 70-percent dark chocolate
- 1 (14-ounce) package extra-firm tofu, excess water drained and tofu patted dry
- 1 teaspoon pure vanilla extract
- 1 teaspoon honey
- 1 teaspoon cinnamon

1. In a medium microwave-safe bowl, heat the chocolate bar in the microwave in 30-second increments until the bar has melted, about 2 minutes.
2. In a blender, blend the tofu, vanilla, honey, cinnamon, and melted chocolate until smooth, about 1 minute, scraping down the sides as needed. Serve as is.
3. The mousse can be stored in an airtight container in the refrigerator for up to 3 days. The mixture may thicken slightly as it cools.

PER SERVING

Calories: 131 | Total fat: 18g | Saturated fat: 4g | Cholesterol: 1mg | Sodium: 11mg | Potassium: 292mg | Magnesium: 57mg | Carbohydrates: 9g | Sugars: 5g | Fiber: 2g | Protein: 6g | Added sugar: 1g | Vitamin K: 2mcg

Cherry Chocolate Cake

Prep time: 10 minutes | Cook time: 2 to 2½ hours on low | Serves 12

- nonstick cooking spray
- 1 cup unsweetened cocoa powder
- 1 cup oat flour, whole-wheat pastry flour, or all-purpose flour
- 1 cup unsweetened dried cherries
- ¼ cup ground flaxseed
- 2 teaspoons baking powder
- ¼ teaspoon salt
- 2 tablespoons extra-virgin olive oil
- 1 large egg
- 2 large egg whites
- 1 tablespoon vanilla extract
- ½ cup granulated sugar
- ½ cup nonfat vanilla greek yogurt
- ¾ cup low-fat or fat-free milk, or plant-based milk, divided

1. Lightly coat the inside of a 6-quart slow cooker with the cooking spray.
2. In a medium bowl, whisk together the cocoa powder, flour, dried cherries, flaxseed, baking powder, and salt.
3. In a separate medium bowl, whisk together the oil, egg, egg whites, and vanilla. Add in the sugar, yogurt, and ¼ cup of milk, mixing thoroughly until no lumps remain. Add the flour mixture and remaining ½ cup of milk, stirring until just combined and incorporated.

PER SERVING

Calories: 173 | Total Fat: 4g | Saturated Fat: 1g | Trans Fat: 0g | Polyunsaturated Fat: 1g | Monounsaturated Fat: 2g | Cholesterol: 16mg | Sodium: 162mg | Carbohydrates: 31g | Fiber: 5g | Sugars: 16g | Protein: 6g

Dark Chocolate Walnut Cookies

Prep time: 10 minutes | Cook time: 1 hour 50 minutes | Serves 4

- ½ cup light brown sugar
- ¼ cup sugar
- 1 large egg
- 3 tablespoons light tub margarine, softened
- 1 teaspoon vanilla, butter, and nut flavoring or vanilla extract
- ¾ cup self-rising flour
- ⅓ cup unsweetened cocoa powder
- 1 cup chopped walnuts, dry-roasted
- Cooking spray

1. Preheat the oven to 350°F.
2. In a medium mixing bowl, stir together both sugars, the egg, margarine, and flavoring just to blend. Using an electric mixer on low speed, beat until well blended.
3. Gradually add the flour to the batter, beating after each addition. Add the cocoa powder, beating on medium speed until well blended.
4. Using a rubber scraper, stir in the walnuts, scraping the side of the bowl as needed.
5. Liberally spray two large baking sheets with cooking spray. Spoon 12 slightly rounded teaspoons of dough onto one baking sheet. Bake for 9 minutes.
6. Meanwhile, on a second baking sheet, spoon out enough dough for 12 cookies.

PER SERVING

Calories: 83 | Total Fat: 4.0 g | Saturated Fat: 0.5 g | Trans Fat: 0.0 g | Polyunsaturated Fat: 2.5 g | Monounsaturated Fat: 1.0 g | Cholesterol: 8 mg | Sodium: 66 mg | Carbohydrates: 11 g| Fiber: 1 g | Sugars: 7 g | Protein: 2 g

Appendix 1 Measurement Conversion Chart

Volume Equivalents (Dry)

US STANDARD	METRIC (APPROXIMATE)
1/8 teaspoon	0.5 mL
1/4 teaspoon	1 mL
1/2 teaspoon	2 mL
3/4 teaspoon	4 mL
1 teaspoon	5 mL
1 tablespoon	15 mL
1/4 cup	59 mL
1/2 cup	118 mL
3/4 cup	177 mL
1 cup	235 mL
2 cups	475 mL
3 cups	700 mL
4 cups	1 L

Volume Equivalents (Liquid)

US STANDARD	US STANDARD (OUNCES)	METRIC (APPROXIMATE)
2 tablespoons	1 fl.oz.	30 mL
1/4 cup	2 fl.oz.	60 mL
1/2 cup	4 fl.oz.	120 mL
1 cup	8 fl.oz.	240 mL
1 1/2 cup	12 fl.oz.	355 mL
2 cups or 1 pint	16 fl.oz.	475 mL
4 cups or 1 quart	32 fl.oz.	1 L
1 gallon	128 fl.oz.	4 L

Temperatures Equivalents

FAHRENHEIT(F)	CELSIUS(C) APPROXIMATE)
225 °F	107 °C
250 °F	120 ° °C
275 °F	135 °C
300 °F	150 °C
325 °F	160 °C
350 °F	180 °C
375 °F	190 °C
400 °F	205 °C
425 °F	220 °C
450 °F	235 °C
475 °F	245 °C
500 °F	260 °C

Weight Equivalents

US STANDARD	METRIC (APPROXIMATE)
1 ounce	28 g
2 ounces	57 g
5 ounces	142 g
10 ounces	284 g
15 ounces	425 g
16 ounces (1 pound)	455 g
1.5 pounds	680 g
2 pounds	907 g

Appendix 2 The Dirty Dozen and Clean Fifteen

The Environmental Working Group (EWG) is a nonprofit, nonpartisan organization dedicated to protecting human health and the environment Its mission is to empower people to live healthier lives in a healthier environment. This organization publishes an annual list of the twelve kinds of produce, in sequence, that have the highest amount of pesticide residue-the Dirty Dozen-as well as a list of the fifteen kinds ofproduce that have the least amount of pesticide residue-the Clean Fifteen.

THE DIRTY DOZEN

The 2016 Dirty Dozen includes the following produce. These are considered among the year's most important produce to buy organic:

Strawberries	Spinach
Apples	Tomatoes
Nectarines	Bell peppers
Peaches	Cherry tomatoes
Celery	Cucumbers
Grapes	Kale/collard greens
Cherries	Hot peppers

The Dirty Dozen list contains two additional itemskale/collard greens and hot peppers-because they tend to contain trace levels of highly hazardous pesticides.

THE CLEAN FIFTEEN

The least critical to buy organically are the Clean Fifteen list. The following are on the 2016 list:

Avocados	Papayas
Corn	Kiw
Pineapples	Eggplant
Cabbage	Honeydew
Sweet peas	Grapefruit
Onions	Cantaloupe
Asparagus	Cauliflower
Mangos	

Some of the sweet corn sold in the United States are made from genetically engineered (GE) seedstock. Buy organic varieties of these crops to avoid GE produce.

Appendix 3 Index

Marlene E. Harris

Printed in Great Britain
by Amazon

37947450R10044